THE LEGACY LEADER

LEADER

Leadership that Creates
Generational Influence

ISBN: 978-0-9876394-2-4

Published by and all communication to:

www.graemelauridsen.com

2024

About the Author

Graeme Lauridsen, a Chief Strategy Officer and Consultant for companies and organisations in Australia, brings a wealth of experience to his role. With a career spanning over forty years, he has coached emerging leaders in the not-for-profit sector and mentored business owners in the marketplace. Today, Graeme is a respected figure in the fields of leadership, strategy, and mentoring emerging leaders, a testament to his deep understanding and expertise.

TABLE OF CONTENTS

PART ONE

Prelude	3
What is Leadership?	7
Everyone is a Leader	19
Vision Creators vs Vision Carriers	29
Vision and Execution	37
Metamodernism and Emerging Generations	49
Culture Incarnate	63
The Futurist and the Strategist	71
The Six Senses of Leadership	77

PART TWO

Lesson 1: Leaders Play the Orchestra	93
Lesson 2: Leaders are Learners	95
Lesson 3: Leaders are Likeable	97
Lesson 4: Leaders are Trained Optimists	99
Lesson 5: Leaders are Accountable	101
Lesson 6: Leaders Think Generationally	103
Lesson 7: Leaders Eat the Frog	105
Lesson 8: Leaders Employ Frog-Eaters	107
Lesson 9: Leaders Ask the Right Questions	109

TABLE OF CONTENTS

Lesson 10: Leaders are Networkers   111
Lesson 11: Leaders Exercise Self-Care   113
Lesson 12: Leaders are Financially Literate   117
Lesson 13: Leaders Create Atmospheres   119
Lesson 14: Leaders Leverage   121
Lesson 15: Leaders are Persuasive   123
Lesson 16: Leaders are Decisive   125
Lesson 17: Leaders Create a Community   127
Lesson 18: Leaders Celebrate Team Wins   131
Lesson 19: Leaders Build Roadmaps   135
Lesson 20: Leaders Keep Promises   137
Lesson 21: Leaders Forgive Quickly   141

PART ONE

THE EIGHT PILLARS OF LEGACY LEADERSHIP

PRELUDE

KEY POINTS

We begin with an overview of "why leadership?" and then introduce the main theme of Legacy Leadership:

"When leadership is multiplied through an organisation, and 'everyone leads', the power of 'leadership everywhere by everyone' creates an explosion of momentum and unlimited growth".

LEGACY:

...something that remains from an earlier time, a benefit that outlasts a lifetime or tenure.

Let's begin by talking about legacy.

Legacy is something of value passed between generations. It may be monetary, property, influence, or reputation. Maya Angelou is quoted as saying, "If you're going to live, leave behind a legacy. Make an impact on the world that can never be erased."

When we link legacy with leadership, we are taking the subject of leadership beyond simply getting things done to getting things done better with influence and meaning. Being a leader in and of itself is a practical outworking of actions and principles that achieve results. A legacy leader adds heart, purpose, intent, and value to the process.

It may be my age, but as a young leader, I focused more on having influence and purpose. Youthful ambition inevitably coloured my goals. However, I am now well into the second half of my career and naturally drawn to the question of legacy. What will I be remembered for? What will I leave behind? Will the impact of my leadership echo into the next generation? Perhaps this book is written for fellow travellers' benefit in the second half of their careers. However, I hope younger leaders will pause and start early in their endeavours to leave a lasting echo for future generations.

But first, let's ask the question: Why leadership? What does leadership achieve? Over the years, I have concluded that leadership gets things done, creates more opportunities, influences more lives, makes more money, and leaves greater legacies.

> *...leadership gets things done, creates more opportunities, influences more lives, makes more money, and leaves greater legacies.*

Leadership is often the missing link to creating growing and lasting legacies. As a leadership mentor, I am amazed how few leaders fully understand its importance. If your business or organisation is struggling, has stalled, or has lost momentum, there is only one cause: a lack of leadership. Throughout this book, I hope to demonstrate that leadership is the primary skill a person needs to leave behind a legacy. If making a difference is your aspiration, you would do well by becoming a lifelong student of leadership.

Personally, I am little more than a student of leadership. I have made more mistakes than I would care to mention. At best, to quote the author, R.C. Sproul, "I am one beggar helping other beggars find bread." In saying this, I can also attest to over forty years of leadership experience. I hope I have inspired more than I have disappointed, and I have helped more than I have hurt. I pray that my many mistakes may serve as an example of pathways best left untrod. I invite you to learn from my errors and be inspired by my wins.

Most of my time is now spent mentoring young leaders. As a mentor and consultant, I have the great privilege of speaking into the lives of hundreds of emerging leaders. When I see the calibre and aptitude of tomorrow's leaders, I am more than hopeful for the future. It is in good hands.

This book takes the discipline of leadership to a higher level. It goes beyond just getting things done and explores the idea that leadership, when fully embraced, has the power to build lasting legacies. Before we begin, let's differentiate between leader and leadership. The term leader mostly refers to a solitary person. Although this book is written for leaders, the subject matter is leadership. Leadership is more than a person; it is a culture, a way of thinking, and a philosophy of achieving desired outcomes.

As you read through The Legacy Leader, you will be introduced to what I believe is one of the most significant, untapped principles of leadership–leadership multiplication. If leadership gets things done, creates more opportunities, influences more lives, makes more money, and leaves greater legacies, what if we could create organisations and businesses where everyone is a leader? The principle of "everyone is a leader" is more than simply saying "everyone leads" but that "everyone leads differently". We will unlock the five types of leadership that make up a leadership culture. Once all five are unleashed in an enterprise, momentum is almost unlimited. This one idea alone is a game-changer. Leadership multiplication will shift your mindset by embracing the idea that leaders don't reproduce followers. The basic multiplication principle implies that followers reproduce followers, but leaders reproduce leaders! It is this primary idea that unlocks the key to creating lasting legacies.

Let the journey begin.

CHAPTER ONE

WHAT IS LEADERSHIP?

KEY POINTS

Before we explore how your leadership can build a legacy, we first need a common understanding of what leadership is. This chapter introduces both a visual and oral definition of what leadership is and the five key components of a successful leader.

I often begin leadership workshops by asking the participants a simple question: What is leadership? On a whiteboard, we write down the answers. A typical list would include:

Example	*Planning*
Team building	*Strategy*
Influence	*Goalsetting*
Being a visionary	*Communication*
Inspiration	*Governance*
Organising others	*Etc.*

Once the board is full, we discuss how we have not written a definition of leadership but a list of what leaders do. In a moment, we will refer to this list as "everything in between." Hold that thought!

Let's discuss what leadership really is. For the sake of us being on the same page as we journey through this book, let's define a leadership model and definition that we can make our common reference point. This model and definition will become the underlying truth upon which every chapter is written. We will begin with a model, which is a visual picture of what leadership is, and then we will add the words.

Here's the model:

Leadership, in its simplest form, always begins with seeing the unseen. It is the ability to visualise a future that is yet to exist. There was a time when Apple Computers and the iPhone didn't exist, but a leader began with a vision. Steve Jobs could see the unseen. The same can be said of Bill Gates with Microsoft, Walt Disney with Disneyland, Elon Musk with Space X and Tesla, and millions of others. The world is filled with visionaries, and those same visionaries change the world. They began with an idea. They then gathered resources, enlisted a team. and turned their unseen into a practical, living reality.

I would venture to suggest that every notable human achievement begins with an idea, a vision, and a leader! Every Olympic champion began with a dream, a vision, and an aspiration to win a gold medal. Then, through self-leadership, they turned their unseen into a reality.

Leadership is to live in the tension between an unseen vision and its fulfilled reality. Leaders begin with a compelling vision, and then by utilising the list on the whiteboard (everything in between), they bring the vision to pass.

Here is the leadership model written in words:

OUR DEFINITION

"Leadership is the ability to create or embrace a compelling vision and bring it to fruition through positively influencing the efforts of others and maximising every resource available."

Leadership is the ability to create or embrace a compelling vision (Seeing the Unseen) and bring it to fruition (Making the Unseen a Reality) by positively influencing the efforts of others and maximising every resource available (Everything In-between)."

We need to deeply understand "what leadership is" before exploring how leadership can be unleashed throughout your business or organisation, igniting unlimited growth and health and creating a legacy. To help us do that, let's break down our definition into the five necessary components that make up the whole picture of leadership.

THE FIVE COMPONENTS OF A LEADERSHIP DEFINITION

1. Clarity of Vision

Leadership is the ability to create or embrace a compelling vision...

Leadership begins with the ability to carry and communicate a clear vision. It is "seeing and describing" the promised land. I remember buying my first computer in the early 1980s. I was an early adopter. Desktop computers were hardly a thing. Yet, it was around 1980 that Bill Gates gave Microsoft, the company he founded, a clear mission: "A computer on every desk and in every home." He could see the promised land. In one small statement, he gave his entire organisation a compelling picture of what could be. The implications of that one dream would create a world vastly different from the one he lived in. He may never have imagined the internet, e-commerce, social media, emails, or YouTube; however, whole industries only exist today because of the proliferation of the personal computer.

When conversing with a leader, I often suggest a date—five, ten, or twenty-five years into the future—and ask, "What do you see?" The clarity of their answer will give me the first sign of their leadership ability. You cannot create what you cannot see.

A few weeks ago, one of my clients, a building company owner, was at a restaurant having lunch with his wife. At a nearby table was a young man wearing his work T-shirt emblazoned with the company logo followed by the words, "...established in 1877". That was 146 years ago. He turned to his wife, pointed out the T-shirt, and asked, "Could our company still exist in a hundred years, and what would it look like?" He began to see a large, flourishing building company. He began to see leadership scholarships in local schools. He began to see a philanthropic arm providing low-cost housing and support for those in need. You cannot lead, build, or create a future you cannot see.

Take a moment to cast your mind to a date five years from now. Write down on a sheet of paper, "What do I see?". You may like to divide your answers into categories: business, family, finances, health, friends, home, etc. Perhaps you could write down the date you would like to retire. Again, what do you see? What kind of home will you be living in? How much savings will you have accumulated? How healthy will you be? Describe your marriage, lifestyle, relationships with loved ones, and hobbies.

I have journaled for most of my life. One of the questions I ask myself at least a few times a week is, "What do I need to see?" That doesn't mean I write something new every few days. But I go to my "goals" page and remind myself of the unseen vision. I remind myself of the marriage, finances, home, family, and business I see. I can see how much I will weigh, the lifestyle I aspire to, the books I will write, how often I will speak at events, and how much I will earn.

Clarity of vision is the first hallmark of a leader. Again, you cannot create a future you cannot see ahead of time.

Throughout this book, we will discuss how to lead emerging generations, which we refer to as the "meta-modernists." One of the hallmarks of millennials and Gen Z is that they aspire to join a cause that is more than just having a job. They need to see what you see, and if it inspires them, they are more likely to enlist in your cause and stay longer if they genuinely believe in it.

2. Social Influence

...positively influencing the efforts of others.

It has been said that people don't leave jobs; they leave managers. One of the fundamental components of a great leader is their social influence, their ability to influence others. Well-known leadership expert John Maxwell defines leadership with this quote, "Leadership is influence—nothing more, nothing less." Think of it this way: the very idea of leadership assumes the presence of followers. The difference between followers and slaves is free will. People get to choose who they follow or who influences them. We all need to ask, why would anyone follow me?

As John Boehner famously said, "A leader without followers is simply a man taking a walk."

When I was a lot younger, I was filled with confidence that people would follow me. I would build strong, growing, and influential organisations. I would gather a gifted and loyal team around me with a shared dream to improve the world. However, over time, I began to understand there is a fine line between confidence and arrogance. I was shocked to find that not everyone liked me. I found that it is in the very nature of leadership to make decisions that would not please everyone. I soon discovered that pleasing everyone all the time is the direct opposite of leadership. My leadership career is littered with people whose disappointment in me is a constant reminder that I cannot always please all the people, and sometimes, I have been the cause of their pain. Over many years of painful lessons, I have learned five primary reasons people follow leaders. In no necessary order, they are:

A. They trust you.

Trust is the primary currency of leadership. However, gaining trust is more than being a moral person or demonstrating integrity. Trust is intentional and specific. Trust lives inside context. What does that mean? Consider this example. My wife trusts me. At the time of writing, we have been married for over thirty-five years. Our trust is deep and committed. However, it is also within context. Can she trust me with chocolate? Well, that may be questionable. If I were her, I would not leave chocolate lying around. The real question is not whether I can be trusted, but what does she need to trust me for? Once we understand that question, we can build a history of trust. Can she trust me to be faithful, tell the truth, never be violent, be a provider, love our children, and have her back?

If you are a leader, have you ever considered what your followers need to trust you for? Perhaps you could ask them. I find my team needs to trust me to have a vision, be kind, reward them for their efforts, include them in decision-making, provide them with the resources they need to do their jobs, act with integrity, and not only have the vision but the capacity to bring it to pass. Trust is the first ingredient to building social influence.

B. They like you.

I'm not sure likeability is more important than trust, but it makes leadership fun. Some of the most outstanding leaders in the world have not necessarily been likeable, but I would suggest that they are the exception to the rule. If people don't like you, you better have a compelling vision and pay your employees well. When asked about his top three leadership principles, Richard Branson, the founder of Virgin, included laughter in his reply. He believed that if you don't enjoy what you are doing, you shouldn't be doing it.

We can learn to be likeable. Just be nice. Be kind. Be positive. Light up the room. Go the extra mile. Acknowledge people. Share the credit when things go well and take the blame when they don't. Practice generosity. Show genuine empathy and compassion. In a nutshell, treat others the way you would like to be treated.

C. They believe in the dream.

If you read Steve Jobs' biography, you will discover that he wasn't always the most likeable person in the room, but he was an expert at describing the Promised Land. He articulated the destination, and people lined up to be on his team. We mentioned earlier that Millennials tend to join a cause more so than take a job. The question you need to ask is this: what does the Promised Land look like? Take a sheet of paper and write down the words, "What is the future I see?" Perhaps write a date on the page—five, ten, fifty, or a hundred years into the future.

As mentioned previously, Bill Gates saw "A computer on every desk and in every home."

D. They feel supported and appreciated.

Social influence begins and ends with empathy. Many years ago, long before the advent of compassionate leave, I experienced a tragedy in our family, resulting in the death of a close family member. I remember calling my employer and asking for an afternoon off to spend with my grieving family. My request was declined for no other reason than to test my loyalty to the organisation. I was in my mid-twenties, and my boss was old-school where the common expectation when in crisis was to "harden up". I lost significant respect for his leadership that day.

Many studies have been undertaken to measure the presence of IQ and EQ in successful leaders. EQ trumps IQ every time. Your first promotion is often achieved through your technical skills, but they will not guarantee you the next. Without going into detail in this chapter, EQ is primarily grounded in a balance between self-awareness and social awareness. Self-awareness is the ability to recognise your emotions and their effect on you and your team's performance. At the same time, social awareness is your ability to read the room and demonstrate support and appreciation.

E. They are provided with the resources to do their job.

The final reason people tend to follow leaders is about being provided with the resources to do their job. Have you ever been given a task and told to "make it happen"? Have you ever told an employee to "make it happen"? Nothing creates discouragement in the workplace more than giving a person a task without the resources required to get it done. As leaders, we can set up our teams to win or lose based on the resources we provide to get the job done. Resources can include the necessary tools and equipment, training and support, and people and technology to ensure their success.

3. Strategy and Planning Skills

...the ability to create or embrace a compelling vision and to bring it to fruition.

The third component of a leadership definition is the ability to make plans and strategies. An old proverb goes: "A vision without a plan is just a dream. A plan without a vision is just drudgery. But a vision with a plan can change the world." Some have elaborated on this proverb by suggesting a vision without the ability to execute is a hallucination. A fundamental leadership role is breaking down the big dream into achievable goals and milestones.

A quick example would be Tesla's story. Tesla's vision is "to create the most compelling car company of the 21st century by driving the world's transition to electric vehicles." Conventional wisdom in their early days was to build a baseline vehicle to capture the sizeable lower-end consumer car space (price tag US$30,000 or less). Instead, they decided to do the opposite. Tesla created the Tesla Roadster, the most luxurious, fully-featured sports car they could afford, with a price tag of over US$200,000.00. Their strategy was to disrupt the market with a stand-out vehicle exceeding anything their competitors would be brash enough to attempt. They followed this with a supply chain strategy, including investing in battery manufacturers.

According to Tom Wright, CEO of Cascade, "Tesla studied and adapted to the industry and business environment they would operate in. They knew their strengths, understood their market position, and built their strategy around their findings instead of following conventional wisdom".

4. Utilisation of Resources

...and maximising every resource available.

I have always believed that the greatest training ground for leadership is how we manage money. In the Biblical narrative, we read of kings and masters who left for faraway lands, giving their servants resources to manage. On their return, they would line up their servants to discover if they had been good stewards of the resources left in their care. Those who had increased the resources were given cities to rule. Those who had buried the resources in the sand were rebuked and dismissed.

You will inevitably struggle to build a successful enterprise if you cannot raise and manage money. We have already spoken about the challenges of IQ and EQ; however, neither will win the day if we do not also embrace financial intelligence. Every leader must be skilled in reading a financial report, understanding profit and loss, and analysing a balance sheet.

5. Result-Oriented

The final component of a leadership definition is being result-oriented. Successful leaders tend to be obsessed with results. They want to know! Management author Peter Drucker says, "You can't manage what you can't measure." In essence, I think he is saying that unless you have a measure of success, how can you quantify your progress? Of course, this can be a negative trait if we become driven by results and more interested in our progress than our people. However, reflecting on our results and potentially changing our course can be a positive practice.

In a strange irony, I wish I had been less and more result-oriented throughout my leadership journey. Less result-oriented in that I would beat myself up too much because of my compulsion to get results. More result-oriented in that I waited far too long to change course when the results were not there.

These five components help us describe our leadership model of living in the tension between the unseen vision and the seen reality and our definition:

> *"Leadership is the ability to create or embrace a compelling vision and to bring it to fruition through positively influencing the efforts of others and maximising every resource available."*

CHAPTER TWO

EVERYONE IS A LEADER

THE FIVE EXPRESSIONS OF LEADERSHIP ACROSS EVERY ORGANISATION

KEY POINTS

This is the deal-breaker chapter. Understanding everyone leads, yet not everyone can be the leader, this chapter explores the five expressions of leadership where everyone fits. The five expressions are not a hierarchy of importance, but a network of leadership where everyone finds their sweet spot.

A quote attributed to Steve Jobs is: "Musicians play their instruments; I play the orchestra." Legacy leaders are rarely solo musicians. To create something that will outlive them, they gather an orchestra and, as much as possible, limit their efforts to the role of conductor. To build a legacy, we need to play the orchestra; if you're going to play the orchestra, you need to know your musicians.

In this chapter, we will take that thought a step further and, building on our previous chapter, demonstrate how everyone in your organisation is a leader.

It may be that you are asking how everyone can be a leader. Wouldn't that mean too many cooks in the kitchen? Perhaps this would be true with a different definition of what leadership is, but let's review our leadership model once again:

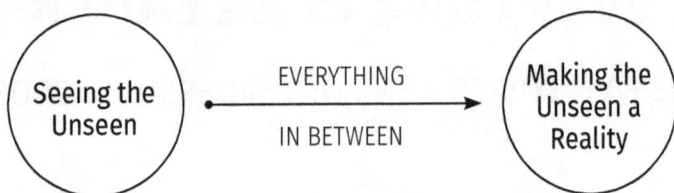

Is there anyone on your team or within your organisation who you do not want to see the vision and then do everything within their power to help it come to pass? Of course not. That makes them a leader. Their primary role is to move the dial from the unseen vision towards the seen reality. That's what leaders do. However, although all leaders share the same goal, they do not share the same role. Each leader moves the dial towards reality differently.

Our research has identified five expressions of leadership necessary to bring a vision to reality. The sole operator must carry all five expressions if a business is a small owner-operator with no extra staff. However, the larger a business grows, the more pronounced each expression is in evolving teams. Here are the five expressions:

Player – Coach – Manager – Executive – Chair

FOOTBALL TEAM

To help understand these expressions, let's consider the metaphor of a football team. Across the team, there are five different leadership expressions, all of which contribute to making the unseen vision a reality, which is to win games.

THE PLAYERS

First, you have the players. They share the overall vision of winning the championship and move the dial towards making the vision a reality by kicking goals. They are on the front line. Often, they are the stars of the show. They don't supervise others, arrange the team bus, or create game plans. Their role is to become the very best athlete they can be.

In your organisation, these could be your salespeople, service providers, receptionists, carpenters, or factory workers. They turn up each day and kick goals!

THE COACHES

Next, you have the coaches. They also share the vision of winning the championship but are not on the field of play. Their role is not to kick goals but to develop a team who can. Whereas the players focus on the game, the coach focuses on the people who play it. They arrange practices and roster the team, help new players learn the skills of the game, and create strategies for team success.

These may be your team leaders, site foreman, leading hand, or supervisors in your organisation. They show up each day, focusing on empowering people and building teams.

THE MANAGERS

Then, you have the managers. The players' focus is on developing skills, the coach's focus is on developing people, and the managers' focus is on developing systems and processes. They book the team bus, employ the driver, organise game days, arrange health and safety, ensure invoices are paid, and oversee all business and administration.

This could be your office manager, HR manager, or accounts manager in your organisation. They, too, play an essential role in leadership. They, too, carry the vision of winning the championship, but they don't express their leadership on the field. Often behind the scenes, they contribute as much as anyone else to moving the dial from unseen vision to seen reality.

THE EXECUTIVE

Players lead by developing skills, coaches by developing people and teams, managers by developing processes and systems, and the executive by developing strategy; they are the people in the board room planning. How can they win the championship next year? Perhaps they create a strategy to find players and coaches who can help them win the championship in five years.

An interesting observation of these expressions of leadership is measuring how far ahead they are planning. Players are often thinking short-term. How can I train today? Am I playing this weekend? How do I prepare for the game? Coaches are thinking months ahead. Perhaps they are developing a team for success throughout the season. Who is injured? Who is on form? How will we prepare for the next five games? Managers are thinking a year ahead. They arrange home games, book hotels, and create systems. The executive team is planning five years ahead. They gauge the current reality and build a longer-term strategy for success.

THE CHAIR

Finally, we have the big-picture person. This may be the owner, CEO, or managing director. Again, the players focus on skills, the coaches on people and team, the managers on processes and systems, the executives on strategy, and the chair on legacy and succession. Their priority is to leave the organisation in a better place than when they received it. Their future planning is generational and succession, not weeks, months, or even years.

THE START-UP JOURNEY

Let's take a moment to explore the five expressions through a start-up journey to help us understand each role. Let's use a plumber as our example. We'll call him Joe.

Joe has worked as a plumber at the same company for several years. He began as an apprentice, completed his apprenticeship, stayed on as a qualified plumber, and eventually became a leading hand with his own team. The time came when he decided to leave the company and start his own.

In the early days, his primary role was as a player. He was on his own. In the evenings, he would look after the manager's role, quoting work, paying bills, and sending out invoices. After six months, he had more work than he could handle. Because his only resource was his time, he hit a ceiling. He had no more time to give.

His only choice was to employ others. He decided to hire an apprentice and another qualified tradesperson. He was now a player/coach, kicking goals and leading the team. Over time, the business continued to grow, and he kept adding to the team, eventually becoming primarily the coach and manager, spending more and more time off the tools and in the office.

Now, it was paperwork that was driving him mad. He was a plumber, not an office manager. It was time to hire a secretary/administrator. Soon, with his team functioning well with a leading hand and an office manager looking after the administration, he could spend more time with his wife, making strategic decisions for the future.

He started as a player, became a coach, and then employed a manager. His primary focus was now strategy. If he continued to grow, open new branches, take on larger projects, and significantly increase his staff, the time would come when he would develop a C-suite executive team and be the big-picture guy, planning for the next generation. This is where his full attention becomes leaving a legacy. He could hand a business to future generations or generate enough profit to support charities and not-for-profit organisations.

Let's make a few observations from this example.

1. A growth ceiling in the business prompted each change. As a player, the ceiling was his time. If he didn't add more staff, the business would stall. He had to become a coach. As a coach, the next ceiling was organisation. There were no systems, health and safety reports weren't current, accounts were out of order, and staff contracts were messy. He had to employ a manager or stop growing. With a manager in place, things began to run far more smoothly. Things became comfortable. He wasn't big enough to make big money, but at least he was more organised. The thing is, he wanted to be successful. He needed strategies that would take him to the next level. He needed advice. He needed a strategic plan, or he would stop growing. Businesses and organisations often hit growth ceilings when a new leadership expression needs to be introduced. Once a strategy team is in place, our plumber has the time to consider his legacy.

2. The best senior leaders have grown through the different expressions. I observe that it is challenging to enter at the higher levels. The best coaches have often been players. The best managers have spent time as coaches. The best strategists have been players and coaches, and they learnt how to become better organised. The best chairs have often experienced each level of leadership across the business or organisation and, therefore, lead with empathy.

3. Many entrepreneurs hit a ceiling at the management level. Often, entrepreneurs hate being stuck in the office. They are at their best in the field, creating new ideas, selling the vision, and making things happen. This being the case, they need to understand the systems and processes required but quickly hire someone else with the aptitude and expertise.

4. These expressions are not a hierarchy of success. Most people happily settle with an expression. I have met many people who are completely satisfied with kicking goals. They don't want to be responsible for supervising others and have no desire to spend their days in an office. For example, some people are outstanding at making sales. They are happy spending their whole life doing this and becoming well financially from it. Some people love coaching others; that's their sweet spot. They are a much better coach than they ever were a player. Then, unbelievable to me, some were born to be managers. They love details, managing systems, and organising things so others can kick goals. When you find where you fit, the key is to be happy to contribute there. If we were to return to our orchestra metaphor, some people are born musicians. Their life goal has been to play the violin in the world's best orchestras. They have no desire to take the conductor's baton.

EXPRESSIONS OVERVIEW.

When we understand that everyone is a leader but leads differently, we can identify each team member within one of the five expressions. They either kick goals with highly honed skills, build people and teams, manage the details, or create strategies for the future. When each expression is fully active in your business or organisation, the big-picture leader is released to dream of what could be. They are free to create legacies.

Here's an overview of each expression:

1. The Player

Focus: Skills

Outcome: Valued team member

Activities: Learn the game, build strengths, and kick goals

Contribution: Fulfil the vision through skills

Planning: Short-term. Days/weeks

Ceiling: Limited time resource

2. The Coach

Focus: People

Outcome: An effective and committed team

Activities: Train, organise, plan, lead

Contribution: Fulfil vision through team

Planning: Short/medium-term, weeks/months

Ceiling: Organisational chaos

3. The Manager

Focus: Organisation

Outcome: Productivity, sustainability, and growth

Activities: Systems, processes, finance and cash flow, organisation, communications, records, HR, Legal, planning, ahead, and policies

Contribution: Fulfill vision through systems and processes, remove chaos, protect the entity, and prepare for scale

Planning: Medium/long-term, One-five years

Ceiling: No time for innovation

4. The Executive

Focus: Strategic planning

Outcome: Strategic plan for the future

Activities: Oversee the health and future of the organ-
                  isation. Culture, innovation, policy change,
                  strategic plan, succession, legal and financial,
                  key appointments

Contribution: Fulfill the vision by strengthening the organisa-
                  tion's health and stability while securing future
                  growth and eventual succession to future
                  generations

Planning: Short/long-term. Six months to fifteen years

Ceiling: Monument vs movement. Protecting what is at
                  the expense of what could be

5. The Chair

Focus: Vision/governance

Outcome: Succession and legacy

Activities: Future vision, build key relationships, dream,
                  make fewer but bigger decisions

Contribution: Seeing the big picture, protecting the dream.
                  Creating Legacy

Planning: Generational

CHAPTER THREE

VISION CREATORS VS VISION CARRIERS

KEY POINTS

In this chapter, we explore the difference between vision creators and vision carriers. If every leader is a visionary, how do you build an organisation of leaders while avoiding the chaos of multiple visions? The key is to differentiate between the two different types of visionaries and celebrate each one equally.

To create a legacy, vision is paramount. A great legacy is always the result of a strong and clear vision. In this chapter, we unpack a dilemma that many organisations face. If everyone is a leader, and every leader has a vision, does that mean an organisation will have multiple visions? Of course, an organisation with multiple visions will inevitably end in tears. I was once asked to consult with a large organisation where the senior leader suffered from burnout. It didn't take long to discover that there was not one clear and definitive vision. In a desire to be a permission-giving leader, everyone was encouraged to create their own vision and run with it. My first management meeting was akin to herding cats. It was utter chaos, and the worst was to come. Each manager had become territorial, and resources were competed for by each team. It didn't take long to understand why the leader suffered from burnout. This chapter addresses this problem by exploring the different types of visionaries. The core principle is this: all leaders are visionaries, but not all visionaries are equal.

In the first chapter, we discussed what leadership is. Here's the model we introduced:

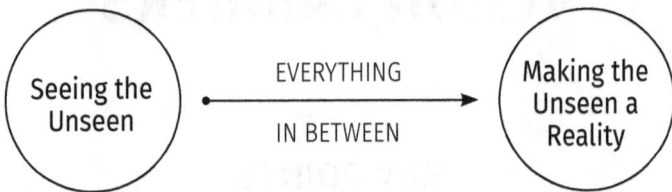

As you can see, leadership at its core is seeing the unseen and then, with everything leaders do, making the unseen a reality. Therefore, if leadership is encouraged across an organisation, and everyone is a leader, that would imply that everyone is a visionary. The proviso here is that although everyone is a visionary, there is only one vision. This may seem a simple observation; however, misunderstanding this truth is one of the key reasons many organisations remain unhealthy.

Let me share a scenario that can be repeated thousands of times. The leadership of a growing business or organisation decides to expand. It may be entering new markets, opening branches, closing unprofitable locations, or restructuring the company for greater productivity. The list is endless. When these new plans are decided upon, they are shared with the rank and file. Middle management receives the news and passes the message on to their teams. All hell breaks loose. The word "they" is repeated in multiple conversations around the water filter. Who do they think they are? What are they thinking? Don't they care about the frontline staff? Do they think customers are going to accept this? Are they out of their minds? They are all in it for themselves. And who are "they"? Whoever has initiated this change. We can see from this scenario that the leadership created a vision, but it has not yet been accepted by those who will need to carry it.

Of course, change management is a skill sadly missing in many organisations, but this is not a chapter about change management. This is about the difference between vision creators and vision carriers.

Recently, I have been involved in a construction company that builds award-winning homes in Australia. One thing I am very clear about is that I am not the vision creator. My role is to understand the vision of the owner (and vision creator) and then to faithfully carry and represent that vision within and beyond the company. I don't get to talk about "they". My constant pronoun is "we". I understand that the business owner is taking the risks, paying the bills, and is responsible for the company's success. He is the "Bill Gates" who saw a computer on every desk and in every home. If I disagree with the vision and want to be the vision creator, I can leave the company and start my own, becoming the vision creator of my dream. There is no in between. I am one or the other, a vision carrier or a vision creator.

Organisations thrive on unity. The best businesses have one vision, not multiple. They don't have a sales vision, manufacturing vision, HR vision, and management vision. They have one vision that is outworked by multiple departments and strategies. Have you ever considered the origins of the word division? Some suggest it originates from two root words: di, or two, and vision. Two visions. It also originates from the Latin divider, which means "to force apart". Either way, division suggests two visions where otherwise united teams are forced apart into separate camps.

The antidote to division is a clear understanding of vision creators and carriers. Here are some keys to releasing this principle through your organisation.

1. Open the boardroom door.

One great key to eliminating the word "they" in your organisation is to invite your teams into the boardroom. Perhaps not literally, but remove the idea that decisions are made in the boardroom and enforced on the factory floor. Recently, I was invited to a lunch meeting where the managing director had invited the sales team to a restaurant where he announced the release of a new suite of products. I know this leader well. He is not only a creative but also a gifted vision creator. He had spent hours putting together these new products and was excited about their potential to help grow the business.

However, he then risked it all. He laid out the new products, discussed the pricing and potential sales pitch, but then did something remarkable. He acknowledged that if the sales team couldn't "see it" and be as excited as he was, he wouldn't proceed. He would invite their further participation until they were all on the same page.

No one in the room doubted that he was the vision creator. He paid their wages. This team had a good understanding that they are vision carriers. However, the creator invited the carriers into the creation process. Every one of those sales reps walked away from the table empowered, excited, and with a genuine belief that they were included in the vision creation process. Their dominant pronoun in their vehicles heading back to work was "we". They were vision carriers who carried the passion and dignity of a vision creator. That was smart! Your vision carriers are more likely to stay with you and accept change if invited into the boardroom to contribute to vision creation.

2. Make the vision clear.

An ancient text reads, "Write the vision and make it plain on tablets, that they may run who read it." If everyone is a leader, everyone needs clarity around the vision. If we don't clarify the vision, we leave room for our teams to write their own. Often, we stop at the brief statement. For example, a computer on every desk and in every home. However, I encourage vision creators to go into more detail. Communicate more than a sentence but less than a page. Some companies call this their manifesto.

If you are a vision creator, take an A4 sheet of paper and write "the future I see..." across the top. Then, begin each sentence down the page with "I see..."

If you are involved in the education sector, it could look something like this:

THE FUTURE I SEE...

- I see a world where every child can access education in a safe and secure environment.

- I see a team of educators who love their job and reap the rewards of making a significant difference in future generations.

- I see a school environment that is fun, uplifting, and devoid of bullying and intimidation.

- I see a school environment where families are integrated into the curriculum, creating a seamless connection between home and school.

- And so on...

Every member of the organisation then has access to the manifesto.

Several years ago, I was consulting with a training institution where every department head wrote a manifesto, with each sentence beginning with "When we're done..." They then came together to align their manifesto with the overall vision.

If we write the vision and make it plain, those who read can run with it.

To enhance this, repeat the exercise, but this time, write down some dates. The future I see ten years, twenty-five years, and fifty years from today. If you plan to hand over the organisation to the next generation, write down your legacy.

As a slight sidetrack, I also encourage those I work with to undertake this exercise on a personal level. Perhaps rewriting the ancient text: "Write the vision and make it plain on tablets, that you may run when you read it." Again, take the sheet of paper and write across the top, "The future I see...". This time, again, put a date. It could be in one, five, or ten years. I undertook this exercise a few years ago using my retirement age: "The future I see at age 67." I then divided the page into sections: "My Family, My Health, My Finances, My Lifestyle, and My Friends." You may have a few more areas to add.

Once you have filled out the page, you begin to ask the following questions: What do I need to do to help this happen? If, at age 67, my mortgage has been repaid and I have a certain level of investments, what do I need to do now to see that happen? If, at age 67, I am fit and healthy and at a certain weight, what do I need to do now to see that happen?

The general principle of this point is to make the vision clear so those who carry it can run with it, including yourself.

3. Share the rewards.

Reward your vision carriers as if it was their idea in the first place. At the heart of becoming a legacy leader is the idea of raising leaders as opposed to followers. Another consideration of this concept is the difference between slaves and sons/daughters. Enslaved people have no sense of ownership. At best, they give their time and energy in return for food and shelter. It is a demoralising existence mostly void of hope. I have long considered that many employees on wages today are treated like modern-day slaves. They earn little more than enough to provide food and shelter for their families without much hope for the future.

Sons and daughters, however, see themselves as part of the inheritance. They believe, "All this will be mine one day, or I will at least share in the inheritance." The sense of reward gives them a greater feeling of hope and perhaps also human dignity.

In his book Good to Great, Jim Collins writes about "the window and the mirror", a concept exemplified by leaders of companies that made the Good to Great transition. In essence, the principle carries the idea that when things go wrong, the glass in front of you is a mirror. You take ownership and responsibility. But when things go right, the glass is a window, and you are looking for someone to whom you can assign credit. By assigning credit to your vision carriers, you build their morale and make them feel like sons and daughters instead of slaves.

4. Create a vision that is big enough and worthy enough for carriers to forego their own.

When a vision carrier joins forces with a vision creator, they sacrifice their right to pursue their vision. They are choosing to pursue your vision above their own. Why would they do that? Because they believe that they can achieve more by chasing your vision than by following your own. They believe you have the vision, the resources, and the strategy to bring it to pass. For some, your vision aligns so closely with their own that they choose not to reinvent the wheel. Why carry the responsibility of such a big vision when they can let you carry that burden and then share in the rewards? Whatever their reason, if you want to attract leaders, you will need a vision big enough to make it worth their while. Quite simply, big dreams attract big people.

The point is that everyone on your team needs to understand the difference between a vision creator and a vision carrier. There can only be one vision creator, even if the vision creator is a team. Once the vision is created, everyone takes on the role of vision carrier. Their main task is to see and interpret the vision within their individual and team roles.

CHAPTER FOUR

VISION AND EXECUTION

KEY POINTS

In this chapter, we explore the two necessary components of Legacy Leadership: Vision and Execution. We link these two with the science of the brain and wrap up with a call to engage 'right brain first, then left'. This understanding will revolutionise how your communication style enhances your leadership.

The brain is a fantastic thing. It is the command-and-control centre for all that we think and feel. It contains about 100 billion neurons and 100 trillion connections (called synapses). Most of us cannot even begin to comprehend what those numbers mean. To put this in some perspective, there is about the same number of neurons in our brain as there are stars in the Milky Way galaxy and as many connectors as there are stars in the universe!

The brain is such an intricate and complex organ that if we are to function effectively as human beings, we need to understand how to best use this vital part of our identity.

Most of us know that research has shown that the brain is divided into two hemispheres, commonly described as the left and right brain or 'the lateralisation of brain function'. The widely accepted theory is that although the two sides of the brain look alike, there is a big difference in how they process information.

The left side is more analytical and orderly, whereas the right is more visual and intuitive.

Nobel Prize winner and Psychologist Roger W. Sperry is credited with first identifying this through his research in the 1960s.

According to his research, the left brain is also connected to logic, sequencing, linear thinking, mathematics, facts, and thinking in words.

The right brain is more connected to imagination, holistic thinking, intuition, the arts, rhythm, nonverbal cues, feeling, visualisation, and daydreaming.

What, you may ask, has this to do with leadership?

Quite simply, a leader leads from both sides of the brain. In this chapter, I hope to demonstrate how leadership communication must be balanced between the right and left brain, or vision and execution.

Consider two sides of a coin.

On one side is the right brain. Let's call that heads. This is where we dream and feel passion for the future. It is where we connect with the people around us and build vision, atmosphere, culture, unity, and momentum. It is where we visualise and imagine a better future.

On the other side is the left brain, which we will call tails. This is where we create systems and processes, read reports, build budgets, and analyse cash flow. We also write policies and ensure the organisation's future stability and security.

Legacy leaders live in the tension between the two sides of the coin. They thrive in the balance between intuition and analysis. They can both imagine and execute a strategy. They see the big picture and then fill in the details. They can embrace both vision and execution.

We can ask: Which side of the brain makes a better leader? Does a left-dominant brain make a better leader than a right-dominant brain, or vice versa? For example, we might assume that an entrepreneur is more right-brain dominant while a CEO or manager is more left-brain dominant.

We would be mistaken!

Although we know the two sides of our brain are different, it does not necessarily follow that we have a dominant side of the brain. We may be right or left-handed, but this does not mean we are right or left-brain dominant.

In 2013, a team of neuroscientists set out to discover whether we can have a dominant side of the brain.

They found that no such proof exists. Using magnetic imaging of over 1000 people, they found that the human brain does not favour one side. Although the two sides function differently, they work together and complement each other. We don't use one side of the brain at a time.

Whether performing a logical or creative function, we receive input from both sides of the brain.

What does this mean in the context of leadership? Simply put, there are no excuses for favouring one over the other. We cannot say we are all visionary and have no time for administration.

Neither can we say that we are all detailed and have no time to inspire passion and vision in our teams. Coins do not have a single side. Legacy leaders take the time to dream and lead intuitively and acquire the disciplines required to automate systems and execute plans.

Legacy leaders take an invisible idea (right brain) and turn the unseen into a reality through the practical principles of business (left brain). They take the abstract (right brain) and create the actual (left brain).

As mentioned, Apple was once an invisible idea in Steve Jobs' mind. Virgin was an invisible idea in Richard Branson's mind. Microsoft was an invisible idea in Bill Gates' mind. The list could go on. However, each embraces balanced strategy and execution to create significant entities that changed how we do business today.

We can only wonder how many great ideas (right brain) have remained a dream because of the lack of execution (left brain) required to make the unseen visible.

Leadership is maintaining *clarity* around what we see and *excellence* around bringing it to fruition.

ROLLING THE COIN

So, we have identified that legacy leaders balance the visual and intuitive with the analytical and orderly. However, there is a third component that brings vision and execution together.

Let's introduce the power of storytelling.

A coin can only have two sides if it also has an edge between them. Imagine a coin in your hand. If I were to ask you to transport the coin across the room without it leaving the floor, you wouldn't push it on its side. Only by rolling it on its edge would you create enough momentum to make the distance.

If 'heads' is visual and intuitive and 'tails' is analytical and orderly, you can see that pushing the coin using only one side will not get much travel. Vision without execution is a pipedream, and execution without vision is drudgery. But balancing the two sides on its edge will create movement.

How do we lead with the balance of vision and execution?

Communication.

The edge of the coin is where communication takes place. Communication takes the two sides and creates traction and momentum.

Communication is the meeting place of vision and execution.

The more competent you become as a leader, the greater the need to become a compelling communicator. Communication takes the intuitive(vision) and the analytical(execution) and brings them to life inside and beyond the organisation.

Both vision and execution are dead without communication! Both the right brain and left brain are lost without a voice.

For this reason, storytelling is one of the most powerful weapons in a leader's communication armoury.

Let's recap. As we have already discovered, the left side of your brain is more analytical and orderly, whereas the right side is more visual and intuitive. While the left side thinks analytically and linearly, the right side tends to be more creative, processing information through imagination and intuition. The left side looks for data and information, whereas the right is more curious, looking for resolution. Images, music, symbols, dreams, and emotions stimulate the right side of the brain.

And here's the interesting note:

Research has shown that the right side of the brain is the pathway to the limbic (emotional) system and quickly becomes emotionally engaged if stimulated. What does that mean? If you want to connect deeply with your audience through communication, don't bury them with facts and figures. Learn how to engage through creativity, imagination, intuition, and emotion.

In 2016, neuroscientist Uri Hasson shared a Ted Talk entitled 'This is your brain on communication'.

In his presentation, he shares the results of his 2010 experiments with fellow neuroscientists Greg Stephens and Lauren Silbert.

They began their experiments by connecting a young woman to a 'functional magnetic resonance imaging' machine and asked her to tell a story about her high school prom. While doing so, they recorded her brain activity. They then asked twelve test subjects to listen to the recorded story while their own brain activity was monitored.

They found that the storyteller's brain activity matched the listeners' brain activity. Take a moment to consider this. Through storytelling, you can begin to resonate with your listeners mentally! There was often a short time lag between the two as the listeners took time to comprehend what was being shared. However, they also found that the test subjects' brain activity began to anticipate that of the storyteller at different points in the story. The listener was predicting what was coming next. What came as a surprise was that the more engaged the listener became, the more they began to predict what was happening next. The better they did in a comprehension test after the experiment.

In response to this research, let me suggest this: When we use storytelling as a form of communication, we engage the right hemisphere of the brain and begin to align our listeners with our message at a much deeper level than if we began with facts and figures.

Therefore, our communication style should be heads first and then tails when communicating to engage our listeners.

EXAMPLES FROM HISTORY

One of history's most outstanding legacy leaders was also an avid storyteller.

Most people would agree that Jesus Christ is one of the most influential leaders in human history. He was a simple tradesman who never travelled more than 200 miles from his birthplace, never used social media, never ran a marketing campaign, and shunned publicity. He never ran for politics, had no military power, and his friends were mostly regarded as the outcasts of society. Yet, almost 2000 years after his death, over two billion people are among his followers.

One of his biographers made this observation:

"Jesus always used stories and illustrations like these when speaking to the crowds. In fact, he never spoke to them without using such parables." (Matthew 13:34)

He told stories. In engaging his followers, his communication style was "heads first, then tails".

His stories are still retold regularly across the world by his followers. Stories like The Prodigal Son, The Good Samaritan, and The Lost Sheep. What is the power of His stories? Like the discoveries of Uri Hasson and his fellow researchers, Jesus' stories aligned his followers with his message. Consider the implications of what this means.

Even 2000 years after these stories were told, they are still feeding the momentum of a global movement. They continue to light up his followers' brains in the same way his brain lit up as he told them.

We can only imagine the magnetic power of his storytelling.

Stories have been used by almost every great business leader of our time. Consider Anthony Robbins as he retells his early days living in a 400-square-foot apartment and washing his dishes in the bathtub. His rags-to-riches story has inspired millions to follow his example and teachings.

Steve Jobs' 2007 iPhone launch is considered the go-to example worldwide of exceptional presentation skills. He walked onto the stage and began with a story—the story of the Macintosh computer, the story of the iPod, and then the story of the iPhone. He had every person in the auditorium on the edge of their seats as his words echoed across the building: "Today, Apple is going to reinvent the phone."

Stories can ignite passion and enthusiasm in those who hear them. Martin Luther King inspired a modern-day revolution with storytelling. Who can imagine a world without his inspirational words:

"I have a dream that one day, on the red hills of Georgia, the sons of former slaves and the sons of former slave owners will be able to sit down together at the table of brotherhood.

I have a dream that one day, even the state of Mississippi, a state sweltering with the heat of injustice, sweltering with the heat of oppression, will be transformed into an oasis of freedom and justice. I have a dream that my four little children will one day live in a nation where they will not be judged by the colour of their skin but by the content of their character. I have a dream today."

For many Western cultures, the history of written words is relatively young. Before the past few centuries, communication was predominantly expressed through oral stories passed from generation to generation.

For this reason, scientists tell us that centuries of story dominance in human interaction have wired the human brain to be predisposed even before birth to think in, make sense of, and create meaning from stories.

We are programmed to prefer stories and to think in story structures. Story is how the brain creates meaning.

This predisposition is strengthened through hearing and telling stories in childhood. I have many beautiful memories of rising early on Saturday mornings and going to sit on my grandfather's knees to listen to his stories. He would share the same ones week after week, but I would love every iteration. In hindsight, I recognise the depth of our interaction as my brain activity began to sync with my lovable grandfather as we journeyed through the Three Bears, Snow White and the Dwarves, and Hansel and Gretel.

WHAT HAPPENS WHEN WE DON'T COMMUNICATE IN STORIES?

Scientists agree that there are two areas of the brain: Broca's area, which is essential for language development and speech, and Wernicke's, which helps us understand speech and use words to express our thoughts.

When we hear a presentation confined to facts and information, these two areas go to work translating the information received into story form so we can find our own meaning. Of course, the potential problem with this is that the story our listeners come up with may not be the same one we want to convey through the data.

An example could be the presentation of a financial report. The data could show a financial loss in a department over the past two years. A person employed in that department could immediately construct a story in their mind of their imminent redundancy. Their mind has rushed ahead in anticipation of their impending departure. They worry about how they will pay their mortgage, provide for their family, and find a new job. However, the story the presenter may have in mind is about the extra investment the company has made in that area over the past two years that will not only forecast future growth but will also be pivotal to the company's future direction and financial success.

Consider it this way: People automatically construct stories to interpret the data their left brain receives. As leaders, we either create the narrative for them, giving a positive and inspiring context, or they will make up their own. Human nature creates the worst possible scenario, so it's better to provide the story than risk your listeners constructing a scenario that misunderstands or misinterprets your message.

THE FEEL-GOOD FACTOR

Stay with me as we go a little deeper to discover why people are more ready to listen to a story than consume facts and figures on their own. Stories feel good. In continuing our journey into the science of communication, scientists have discovered that when we listen to an inspiring story, our brains release chemicals that help us to pay attention and remember.

Just think of that the next time you watch a movie. Chemical explosions are bursting through your brain! Well, maybe that's a slight exaggeration.

The point is:

- cortisol is causing you to sit up and pay attention.

- oxytocin connects you to the characters, causing you to bond and build trust with the good guys.

- dopamine is keeping you focused and engaged.

- endorphins are adding the feel-good factor.

As with a movie, it's the same with your listeners when you communicate through story. It is incredible how powerful storytelling can be when you utilise its power through your leadership communication.

So far in this chapter, we have established that leadership requires a balance between vision and execution, right brain and left brain, and that the key to leading through this tension is communication and storytelling, giving context to our data. Heads first, then tails.

Let's finish this chapter with one piece of advice.

Stop. Being. Boring!

An old communication quip says, "If you don't strike oil in the first fifteen minutes, stop boring." It is true. People will forgive you for almost anything, but they will not forgive you for being boring. As a leader, work hard to ensure your communication comforts the afflicted and afflicts the too comfortable. What is the best way to accomplish that? A story!

Consider this statement: As a legacy leader, the higher you rise in your leadership role, the more time you spend on communication.

Many leaders of legacy organisations will find that the larger their organisations grow, the more time they spend thinking and communicating. One leadership description is expressed in the statement, "I would rather get ten people to do the work than do the work of ten people." Whether you have ten, a hundred, or a thousand people doing the work, most of your role becomes thinking and communicating.

The higher you rise in your leadership role as a visionary and master of execution, the more significant proportion of your time is spent in communication.

CHAPTER FIVE

METAMODERNISM AND EMERGING GENERATIONS

KEY POINTS

In this chapter, we explore how millennials and Gen Z have changed the fabric of the workplace. We have moved from modernism to postmodernism to what is now being coined metamodernism. Most people entering the workplace today are millennials and Gen Zers, and they come with a different set of leadership expectations. If we are to succeed in this new era, we need to change how we do leadership and how to communicate through story.

As Steve Jobs demonstrated, legacy leaders play the orchestra. They don't just build companies and organisations; they build teams that build companies and organisations. The essence of a legacy includes creating something that will outlive our lifetime. For this reason, we not only build teams but also enlist emerging generations. This chapter will explore how leadership must adapt to empower emerging generations. The old ways don't work anymore. Things have changed!

So, what has changed? Let me introduce you to the meta-modernists.

THE ERA OF METAMODERNISM

When discussing changing leadership trends, one description could be that we have shifted from postmodernism to metamodernism. So, what is metamodernism? Luke Turner wrote in his article "Metamodernism: A Brief Introduction" at metamodernism.com:

> "Whereas postmodernism was characterised by deconstruction, irony, pastiche, relativism, nihilism, and the rejection of grand narratives (to caricature it somewhat), the discourse surrounding metamodernism engages with the resurgence of sincerity, hope, romanticism, affect, and the potential for grand narratives and universal truths, whilst not forfeiting all that we've learned from postmodernism."

Modernist thinking of the early 20th century generally embraced the search for an abstract truth of life. The postmodernist countered this approach with the belief that there is no universal truth, abstract or otherwise. The truth was in the eye of the beholder. The metamodernist introduces a new era that embraces modernism and postmodernism without apparent contradiction.

Again, in the words of Luke Turner,

> "...rather than simply signalling a return to naïve modernist ideological positions, metamodernism considers that our era is characterised by an oscillation between aspects of

both modernism and postmodernism. We see this manifest as a kind of informed naivety, a pragmatic idealism, a moderate fanaticism, oscillating between sincerity and irony, deconstruction and construction, apathy and affect, attempting to attain some sort of transcendent position, as if such a thing were within our grasp. The metamodern generation understands that we can be both ironic and sincere in the same moment; that one does not necessarily diminish the other."

The metamodernist calls us to enter a new era where cynicism and structural distrust are balanced with an inner desire to be part of something meaningful. It may be that many are waking up to an empty bath. Having thrown out the baby with the autocratic, authoritarian bathwater, they now feel the ache of a life without meaning, cause, and lasting significance. They are not willing to unquestioningly trust structures and authority but are more pragmatic. They realise that to make a positive difference in society and build a legacy, they cannot travel alone.

Through this societal change, we are presented with an opportunity to introduce a fresh and innovative approach to leadership. An approach that is not an inferior style moulded to a changing culture but leadership in its most inspirational form. A leadership style is not top-down, autocratic, or authoritarian but about the team where everyone has a voice and everyone leads. This "everyone leads" approach is not a pathway to anarchy but a recognition of the different expressions of leadership that, when fully understood, create a leadership culture where everyone shares the vision, the responsibility for bringing it to pass, and the credit for success. This is the kind of leadership that builds legacies. Leadership that is everyone, everywhere, and everything. Leadership that is reimagined in a way that is relevant to a metamodernist workplace.

WHO ARE THE METAMODERNISTS?

As I settled into the barber's chair, I was introduced to the extremely funky Sarah, the young millennial who would be cutting my hair. Sarah had recently opened Lost and Found, a local barber shop in Albury, about three hours north of Melbourne, Australia. The décor was fresh and alternative, the atmosphere was welcoming, and Sarah was fashion-conscious and creative (is that a thing?). As our conversation progressed, I soon discovered Lost and Found was more than a barbershop. It was a story. A narrative. A greater cause.

The dream was to create a hub, a safe, creative space in the community where we can all call one another family. Although Sarah had a passion for hair and fashion, her venture was only a small part of a more significant cause to build lifelong connections in her hometown where lost and found stories could find an expression.

As I came to know Sarah and others like her, I became increasingly aware that Millennials (those born between approximately 1977 and 1995) and Gen Z (generally regarded as those born from 1996 to the early 00s) see the world very differently from my Gen X and baby boomer contemporaries. As citizens of the metamodernist era, they are not rebelling from an authoritarian society or willing to conform to societal norms. They desire to join a cause. They desire more than a job, an income, or a role description. They are ready to sign up for a cause, an adventure.

At the time of writing, many of our existing leadership principles are geared towards Gen X and boomers, yet millennials are the largest segment of the workforce. Gen Zers are now graduating from university and are already the fastest-growing generation in the workforce and the marketplace. This will have a significant impact on how we approach leadership.

THE MILLENNIALS ARE TAKING OVER, AND GEN Z ARE HOT ON THEIR HEELS.

Consider some of the findings of the 2016 Deloitte Millennial Survey.

The survey found that "one in four millennials intend to quit their job and join a new organisation or do something different in the next twelve months. That figure increases to 44% when the time frame is expanded to two years. Only 16 percent of millennials see themselves with their current employers a decade from now."

Imagine losing a quarter of your workforce every year! That would devastate momentum and denigrate culture. How do we build a legacy with that level of staff turnover?

The easy response to these statistics would be to point out millennials' lack of loyalty and say this is their fault. But before we jump to that conclusion, consider this finding, which was also included in the Deloitte survey: Younger professionals intending to stay with their organisation for more than five years are twice as likely to have a mentor as those who do not (68% to 32%, respectively).

In other words, this is not just a millennial problem but a leadership problem. Many millennials crave coaching and personal development, and if it is not available at their current organisation, they'll move somewhere where it is. Millennials and Gen Z are changing the fabric of the modern workplace.

In brief, they are cause-driven, looking for mentors, collaborative in work style, looking for constant feedback, and needing financial reward to alleviate their significant student debt.

Hence, one of the most significant challenges facing leadership today is the effective management of millennials and Gen Z. The future of leadership needs to be vastly different from its history if organisations are to maintain growth and momentum and build legacies. Those who embrace change positively will thrive, while those organisations that maintain the status quo will die.

METAMODERNISM, LEADERSHIP, AND COMMUNICATION

In a recent survey by Randstad and Future Workplace, Gen Z and millennials responded that the most important quality of a leader is communication.

Communication was the standout attribute and rated higher than honesty, confidence, and being approachable.

Why is communication such an essential quality for young professionals today? Perhaps more than any previous generation, today's young people have grown immersed in stories. It is their second language. From television stories to computer games, social media, and reality shows, almost all communication is in the context of a story. It should be no surprise that when they arrive in the workplace, they are looking for a story to give them a framework to find their place.

When millennials and Gen Z rate communication highly, they ask to be treated as people. "Don't just manage us. Lead us. Talk to us. Listen to our ideas and opinions. Give us a seat at the table. Don't just utilise us; mentor us. You will eventually lose us if all you do is use us." In other words, "Communicate!"

Today's legacy leader is a storyteller. However, it is one thing to be a storyteller and another to know which stories are important.

Let's explore the stories metamodernists yearn to be part of.

HOW TO COMMUNICATE WITH YOUR MILLENNIAL

There are three stories millennials and Gen Z are looking to hear from their leaders.

STORY ONE: YOUR STORY

One of the key differentiators the Centre for Generational Kinetics has found in its research into Gen Z is their deeper desire to make a difference in the world. They prefer a job that makes a positive impact in some way. They are eco-conscious and concerned about humanity's impact on the environment.

Before they join your team, they need to know and embrace your story.

They are not coming to work for you but to join your cause.

Admittedly, if you pay them well, they may come on board for a season but soon go when someone else is prepared to pay them more. Money is important to them but not as important as purpose.

We need only look at the recent (2019) rallies inspired by Greta Thunberg demanding a global warming emergency. Gen Z rallied to change the world for the better. The demonstrations in Hong Kong (2019) are another example, primarily led by millennials, of rallying to a cause for democratic freedom.

What is your story? What is the cause? What moved you to start the business? What problem are you solving? What monster are you slaying? What will you be remembered for? In brief, what is the legacy?

If you don't have a compelling story, some of your best potential team members will find their way to someone with one. But if your story is authentic and genuinely inspirational, you will never be in need of the best candidates to join your team.

STORY TWO: OUR STORY

Millennials and Gen Z have also been labelled the Collaborative Generation. When asked by the Randstad survey what enables them to do their best work, 56% responded, "The people I work with." This longing to collaborate goes beyond good work relations; they want to own the story.

Let's talk about gaming.

It would be hard to find a young person in the workplace today who has not been exposed to gaming. Over time, gameplay has evolved toward two storylines: linear and nonlinear.

Linear gameplay is games in which a player cannot change the storyline or the ending. Each challenge leads to the next, and the game is won when all the levels are completed.

Nonlinear gameplay offers branching storylines, also referred to as an 'interactive narrative' where the player can choose how the storyline will unfold, some even leading to multiple endings.

Of course, building a nonlinear storyline requires a lot more effort and expense; however, for the player, having some control over how the story unfolds and ends can be much more rewarding.

Successful leadership in the future needs to embrace a nonlinear style.

Top-down and dictatorial hierarchies are an anathema to this generation.

They don't look for a workplace where they are given tasks to complete each day toward an outcome they may not care about.

It would be a mistake to think they are just being rebellious or want only their own way. It's much deeper than that. They do want to be part of a meaningful story. They desire to play a part in creating the storyline. If they have a sense of ownership around how the story ends, they are far more likely to work harder and stay for the finish.

I have experienced two types of leaders; let's be honest, both can succeed.

1. *Those who 'share the vision'.*

The first is one who regularly shares their vision with the team. They have team and staff gatherings where they share the 'future they see'. They are often inspirational and charismatic. Once they have shared the vision, everyone is given a role to fill. If we all play our part, the vision will become a reality. Each player is playing a linear game.

2. *Those who share 'ownership of the vision'.*

This leader also shares the vision regularly. They, too, are often inspirational and charismatic. However, there is a difference. Instead of sharing the 'future they see', they invite the team to create the 'future we see". Of course, as an owner, the outcome is his or hers to call, but if everyone can play a nonlinear game, the buy-in and loyalty factor will increase significantly. In this leadership style, everyone can have a voice. Everyone has skin in the game. It is 'our story'.

A TALE OF TWO PRESIDENTS

An example of this concept is seen in the different slogans two presidents used to come to power in the United States.

In 2016, Donald Trump won the presidency with the slogan, "Make America Great Again."

His vision inspired enough voters to back him and win the White House.

Eight years earlier, a different slogan brought another president to power. Barak Obama joined the race, and his followers would chant three words at his rallies: "Yes, We Can."

Both came with T-shirts and caps, but let's ask which slogan most appealed to Millennials.

In 2008, Obama came to power with 66% of the eighteen to twenty-nine-year-olds' vote.

In 2016, Trump came to power with 28% of the eighteen to twenty-nine-year-olds' vote.

Millennials, and even more so Gen Z, desire to be included in writing the story. Invite your team to help construct the storyline of the future. What will the future look like? What are the milestones we will reach along the way? What is our great cause? What difference can we make? How will we all feel when we achieve the vision?

The leader who shares their story will attract followers. However, the leader who creates our story will attract leaders.

STORY THREE: THEIR STORY

It may come as a surprise that according to the Randstad Survey previously referred to, 32% of millennials and 37% of Gen Z aspire to lead their own company in the future. We have already written that millennials crave personal development and coaching. They are increasingly ambitious and will value any leader who helps them in their personal growth.

Perhaps more than any previous generation, they see themselves as their story's main character. They have grown up with social media. The 'story' option on Facebook and Instagram is an example. Viewers can follow your story as the day unfolds. Imagine explaining that to your grandparents twenty years ago. They would never believe that in the future, people will photograph and video their day so strangers can watch their life in 'story form'. To be honest, they would likely have difficulty understanding why.

The point is that today's young people are passionate about their stories. They are looking for leaders who will permit them to have their dreams and help prepare them for a bigger future.

How can we give them that support? I suggest three ways:

1. _Constant feedback._

Once a story is posted, what is every Instagrammer hoping for? Likes and comments. The more likes and comments they receive, the better they feel about themselves. Historically, most employees would receive an annual performance review. Let us repeat that... ANNUAL performance reviews. Instagrammers are checking for a performance review every few minutes. If we wait twelve months to offer feedback to millennials and Gen Zers, we will be at least eleven months too late. They will be long gone!

Constant feedback is now the expectation.

2. *Help craft their story.*

Give your team permission and the opportunity to craft their own story. Let them share it with you. Ask them, "Where do you see yourself in five years, ten years, or beyond?" What difference do you want to make? How can I make space for you in 'our story'?"

Offer advice. Give them further training. Be the Obi-Wan Kenobi to their Luke Skywalker.

Be prepared to be in the rolling credits of their movie.

This goes against the grain for many leaders and entrepreneurs. Most have big egos and work long hours to write their own stories, but understand this: If we cannot champion the stories of our team, we will not keep them for long.

Here is the big lesson.

Legacy leaders of tomorrow will be those who master the art of weaving 'my story, our story, and their story' into one epic masterpiece where everyone feels like they are part of history.

3. *The story of us.*

Most millennials would quickly recognise the names Ross, Rachel, Joey, Chandler, Phoebe, and Monica. The Friends sitcom played a significant role in providing a background narrative for their generation. Boomers had their own sitcom version called Cheers. Cheers was a bar where 'everyone knows your name'.

Underlying our call to make 'story' an essential part of your communication style is a much deeper storyline that can become the glue that keeps your team together. Every generation long for the story of us. The 'story of us' is a culture built on the premise that everyone belongs here.

The story of us is built upon the promise of finding our tribe. The security of knowing you will not be bullied or intimidated—the joy of being celebrated.

· · · · ·

Legacy leadership is not a leader with loyal followers but a community of leaders gathered around a vision created primarily by a vision creator and then crafted by the tribe.

CHAPTER SIX

CULTURE INCARNATE

KEY POINTS

Legacies are built on the foundation of a healthy culture.
Culture is made up of shared beliefs, ideas, customs,
language, actions, habits, and values of a particular group
of people. Get these right and you create the possibility of
creating something that will influence others for generations
to come.

Culture has been a buzzword in leadership circles for many years, and for good reason. I've called this chapter Culture Incarnate to add one thought to this vast topic. Before we head there, let's first briefly describe what culture is. Most definitions include the shared beliefs, ideas, customs, language, actions, habits, and values of a particular group of people. However, for this chapter's purpose, I will simplify it and reduce the definition to just a few words: Habits of the heart.

Several years ago, I spoke to the leadership team at a large pharmaceutical company in Melbourne, Australia, about company values. Everyone knew the company values because they were written on the wall. The problem was that they were not written on people's hearts. The culture within an organisation is not determined by the seven values written on the wall but by the habits, actions, language, beliefs, and norms demonstrated by the people who work there. I have heard it said that "culture trumps vision every time", and I agree. When we interact with a business or organisation, we don't walk away impacted by the vision statement on the wall but by the people's words, actions, and behaviours. It is not only what we do that influences others, but who we are. When I suggest that culture reflects "habits of the heart", I propose that culture is an inside-out job. It is incarnate, which means embodied in human form.

Here, we consider five key ideals for building a strong culture in your organisation.

THE POWER OF THEREFORE

The first principle of instilling culture throughout your organisation is to take your core values and write "therefore" after each one. Of course, this implies that you have already chosen your values. Let's cover that first.

Values in an organisation are the core principles upon which culture is established. How those values are chosen is essential. Many leadership teams make the mistake of simply reflecting their own personal values. Of course, this has merit. However, I lean more towards having two sets of values: corporate and personal.

Consider this. I am a human being. I have a personal culture, often reflected by my upbringing, background, and personal values. I may then join a team in an organisation, and as part of my onboarding, I am introduced to the company culture made up of a group of values. The expectation, of course, is that I will embrace and represent these values throughout my professional life. Do I then cancel my personal culture and replace it with the new company culture? Of course not. I hope a level of alignment and commonality will enable me to embrace both personal values and those embedded within the organisation.

How are the values within an organisation chosen?

I often ask leaders to answer five questions concerning their business:

Who are we?

What do we do?

Who do we help?

What do they need?

What difference do we make?

Who we are describes our values and story. What we do clarifies what we offer to the marketplace. Who we help describes our ideal client. What they need focuses our products and services on the real problems we are solving, and proving the difference we make holds us accountable for successfully making a difference in their lives. It is a powerful exercise. It enables us to dive deeply into our customers' needs and expectations.

Having completed this exercise, we can then ask another question. What kind of values would enable us to solve the problems our ideal customer is facing successfully? So, these are not the personal values shaped by our upbringing but the specific values shaped by the needs of the people we serve. For example, our values may include deep compassion and empathy if we serve people experiencing homelessness. Or if we entertain children at birthday parties, our values may consist of happiness and responsibility. You get the picture.

Back to the power of therefore and culture incarnate.

Once you have established the values that will dictate your culture, preferably with your team, write "therefore" after each. What is the "therefore" there for? To ensure your values leave the wall and are embedded into human form. Let's take one as an example. As mentioned above, you entertain children at birthday parties. One of your values is responsibility.

Responsibility: Therefore, our staff are never alone with a child, bathroom visits are always accompanied by a second adult, and we always take responsibility for the personal safety of each child in all activities at all times.

The power of "therefore" enables us to have clear guidelines for our staff to which we can add accountability.

Consider taking a sheet of paper and writing your business values down the left side of the page, followed by the word, therefore. After that, write down the customs, language, actions, and/or habits that will give an action plan for each value.

VALUE-BASED CONVERSATIONS

Clearly defined values accompanied by corresponding actions and behaviours give us a narrative for giving direction and correction. Let's take our children's birthday party business as an example. Perhaps you have hired a new team member who entertains as a clown at parties. You share your company culture as part of their onboarding, including each 'therefore'.

At their first birthday party, you notice your new clown accompanying a child to the bathroom. This is cause for a conversation. However, your conversation need not be based on suspicion but on culture. You quickly remind them of the company culture document they signed upon employment and ask them to honour each value by following the guidelines following the 'therefore'. Value-based conversations make corrective action less personal and more professional. Essentially, you are saying we don't do things that way here. It's not who we are. We follow the guidelines.

I worked with a customer-focused company whose staff regularly interacted with the public. One of their chosen values was happiness. Their 'therefore" described greeting people with a smile, portraying a cheerful demeanour, and maintaining an atmosphere of happiness and joy. One employee would regularly arrive at work depressed. They would sit in a corner with their head down, hiding behind their hair. When approached about their demeanour, they responded with how they felt at the time. They shouldn't have to fake happiness if they are sad.

Of course, their response contained an element of truth. However, this was not a personality-based conversation but a value-based conversation. They were not asked to fake happiness but to represent the organisation's culture.

THERMOMETER OR THERMOSTAT

Another principle behind making culture incarnate is observing the difference between a thermometer and a thermostat. A thermometer can measure the temperature, while a thermostat can adjust it. A thermometer will tell you if it's too cold, too hot, or just right. A thermostat will identify things that are too cold and warm them up or too hot and cool them down. To create culture, we need thermostats, not just thermometers.

Let me explain.

Imagine that excellence is a cultural value in a business. Therefore, we always maintain a clean and tidy environment. One morning, there was a storm overnight, and a rubbish bin had spilled its contents across the car park.

The thermometer people will arrive at work and inform everyone about the mess in the car park. The thermostat people will immediately pick up the rubbish, maintaining a clean and tidy environment.

Again, imagine honour is a cultural value in a business. Around the water cooler, one employee develops a habit of gossiping about colleagues. A thermometer will walk away saying nothing, or worse, join in the narrative. A thermostat will speak up, perhaps having a private conversation explaining, "We don't do that here."

Thermostat employees create a self-correcting culture. Leadership no longer needs to address negative behaviours repeatedly. The team self-corrects. That is the power of the thermostat.

CITIZENS OR RESIDENTS

I am a New Zealander living in Australia. Officially, I am a New Zealand citizen, but I am classified as a resident of Australia. I happily contribute positively to Australian society, but if we were to go to war, I would fight for New Zealand. I love living in Australia, but I'm cheering for the All Blacks when Australia plays New Zealand on the rugby field—no doubt about it.

Regarding culture, be aware that not everyone on our teams will be citizens. Some will have their citizenship elsewhere but remain good, contributing residents. Why is this important? It is all about our expectations of people and who we promote.

Take a moment to consider the different employees and team members in your organisation. You will be able to identify the citizens and the residents very quickly. Citizens are those people who are all in. They happily stay late when needed. They represent the company in its best light all the time. They reflect the company culture. They are vision carriers and vision casters, sharing the vision with everyone they meet. Residents are also good people. But they may have an eye on the clock and are looking to leave for home when their shift ends. They may work hard, but their primary motivation is to make enough money to support their family. They understand the vision and values, but they may not defend them. They're good people, but they are not all in.

Here's the point. We need both citizens and residents. In very rare cases, you may have an organisation with only citizens on your team, but most times, you will have both. The key is to look after your residents but promote your citizens. Both citizens and residents are vision carriers, but it will be your citizens who are vision casters. Put another way, residents tend to be thermometers, and citizens tend to be thermostats.

On a positive note, the Australian government has recently passed legislation making it easier for New Zealanders to become Australian citizens. That's the key. Identify your residents and then make it easy for them to become citizens. The easiest way to do that is to affirm and celebrate positive behaviour. See if you can catch your residents doing the right thing. Thank them for their contribution. Honour them in front of their peers when they go the extra mile. When we value people, they feel more valuable. When residents feel more valuable to the organisation, they feel a sense of ownership. When they increase their sense of ownership, they move towards citizenship.

Before we move on, we need to identify a third category: the detractors. These are the people who undermine the vision. Where residents may be passive concerning vision and culture, detractors oppose them. They tend never to lose an opportunity to share their negative opinions. Most times, deportation is your best option. Of course, some may change their attitude and move towards residency, but in my experience, most do not. My advice is to hire slowly and fire fast. Most employment contracts include a probationary period, often six months. If you want to protect your culture, take that six-month window and test your new employees. Do your best to identify your potential citizens, residents, and detractors. And fire fast!

LEADING FROM THE FRONT

Finally, be a leader who demonstrates culture. Leaders set the bar. If you're the first to arrive at work, and the storm has blown rubbish across the car park, consider doing the cleanup yourself. Of course, you could call the janitor or find a lowly employee, but you would miss an opportunity to set the bar. The truth is, we don't reproduce rules but behaviours. If you desire a friendly culture, are you friendly? If you desire a corporate dress code, are you setting the standard? If you desire a fun and vibrant workplace atmosphere, are you fun to be around? Be the thermostat.

· · · · ·

In closing, why is culture so important to legacy leadership? A self-perpetuating culture will maintain momentum and growth without your presence being required. When a company reflects a thermometer, you arrive at work and turn on the heater to warm things up or the air conditioner to cool things down. You need to be hands-on. Present. However, when a company reflects a thermostat, the temperature automatically warms up or cools down when required. Choose the right values with clear action points following your 'therefore', and your thermostat will maintain positive momentum.

CHAPTER SEVEN

THE FUTURIST AND THE STRATEGIST

KEY POINTS

The most important relationship for a legacy leader is the partnership between the futurist and the strategist. The futurist sees the future and builds the team to bring it to pass. The strategist sees the team and their gifts and provides the strategy that will position them to bring the vision to pass.

In 1998, Tim Cook joined Apple Computers and, over time, became the senior vice president of worldwide operations. His ability to manage Apple's complex operations, from supply chain management to sales and beyond, caught the eye of Steve Jobs, Apple's co-founder and then-CEO. Their partnership became a defining element of Apple's growth and resurgence in the early 2000s. Under Jobs' visionary product direction and Cook's operational strengths, Apple developed and released successful products like the iPod, iPhone, and iPad.

Over time, Cook took on more responsibilities. When Jobs was diagnosed with a rare form of pancreatic cancer in 2004, Cook filled in during Jobs' medical absences, temporarily assuming leadership roles. In 2009, he served as Apple's interim CEO while Jobs was on medical leave.

Steve Jobs was a futurist. He could foresee what consumers wanted even before they knew it themselves, and he pursued his vision with relentless passion. His charisma, storytelling prowess, and demand for perfection were legendary. On the other hand, Tim Cook is a strategist known for his calm demeanour, operational expertise, and deep understanding of the intricacies of global supply chains. While Jobs focused on product innovation and big-picture strategy, Cook ensured the company's operations ran seamlessly. This relationship allowed Apple to innovate rapidly while ensuring its products reached consumers efficiently. This is a classic example of the futurist and strategist working together.

While they had different personalities, Jobs and Cook shared core values that shaped Apple's culture. Both believed in the power of simplicity, the importance of product excellence, and the need to place the user at the centre of every decision. In August 2011, the inevitable transition happened. Jobs resigned as CEO of Apple due to his deteriorating health, recommending Tim Cook as his successor.

In chapter two, we introduced the five expressions of leadership within every organisation. In this chapter, we focus on the roles of chair and strategy. Although not every chair is a futurist, I have concluded that one of the greatest keys to building a legacy business is the partnership of a futurist and a strategist working closely together.

Compelling dreams can be achieved when a discerning strategist joins a visionary futurist. It is worth mentioning that a futurist often has strong strategist skills and vice versa. The problem arises when they try to do both. They may be capable of both;

however, it is better to split the roles when an enterprise reaches a certain size. One person primarily dreams of the future promised land, while the other develops the roadmap to get there.

Futurists provide the inspiration and forward-thinking ideas necessary for innovation, while strategists offer the structured approach and practical execution needed to bring these ideas to fruition.

Of course, Steve Jobs and Tim Cook are not the only ones who have demonstrated this partnership. Here are a few others:

STEVE BALLMER AND BILL GATES

Steve Ballmer attended Harvard University, where he met Bill Gates. While Gates dropped out to start Microsoft, Ballmer graduated in 1977 with degrees in applied mathematics and economics.

Ballmer began his career at Microsoft as an assistant to the president over four decades ago, though his role at the time was more of a business manager for the fast-growing software maker. He was the strategist to the futurist Bill Gates. Rising through the ranks to eventually become its president and CEO, he succeeded Gates. Ballmer stepped down as CEO in 2014, the same year he bought the Los Angeles Clippers basketball team.

A former Microsoft assistant, he became the fifth-richest person in the world, only one spot behind Gates on the Bloomberg real-time list of the world's richest people, with his wealth exceeding $117 Billion. He was Microsoft's 24th-ever employee, joining in 1980. This is another example of the futurist and strategist working together.

WALT AND ROY DISNEY

Another example is the partnership between Walt Disney and Roy O. Disney, co-founders of The Walt Disney Company. Walt Disney, the creative futurist, conceptualised iconic characters and groundbreaking theme parks. At the same time, Roy O. Disney, as the strategist, focused on financial management, strategic planning, and ensuring the company's operational success. This partnership transformed Disney into the global entertainment juggernaut it is today.

Walt and Roy, the visionary futurist and the pragmatic strategist, complemented each other perfectly. While Walt was the imaginative force behind groundbreaking concepts and creative worlds, Roy provided the steadfast business acumen that turned dreams into reality. Their harmonious collaboration ensured that the magic they envisioned could flourish within the boundaries of financial stability.

Central to their success was a shared vision that extended beyond individual desires. Walt's creativity needed Roy's organisational abilities to make things work.

The journey of the Walt Disney Company was not without its challenges–from early financial struggles to complex creative endeavours. However, Walt and Roy stood united, weathering storms as a team.

For every futurist leader, finding your "Roy" means recognising the partnership that will complement your skills and share your passion, offering a yin to your yang. This partnership isn't just about balance; it's about unleashing your full potential.

Every futurist needs to find their Roy.

Having a "Roy" by your side is a game-changer in the complicated business world. It means delegating operational strategy to someone who understands your goals and values so you can fulfil the vision. Your "Roy" allows you to channel your energy into your true passions while they expertly navigate the rest.

The stories of Steve Jobs and Tim Cook, Bill Gates and Steve Ballmer, Walt and Roy Disney are not just stories of brothers or colleagues but lessons in collaboration's transformative power. As futurists, discovering your "Roy"–a strategic partner who complements your strengths–can be the catalyst that propels your dreams toward remarkable success and legacy.

If you cannot yet employ a strategist full-time, you may want to consider finding a fractional employee. A virtual CFO or GM can bring the strategic skills required to your team and help you reach the next level as a business or organisation.

FIVE KEYS TO FINDING YOUR ROY

PERSONAL COMPATIBILITY

The first attribute of your futurist/strategist partnership is personal compatibility. You must enjoy working together. You will be spending a lot of time with this person, and they will likely challenge your perspective and decisions. You are not employing a "yes person" but someone who will often push back. They will sometimes feel like an antagonist, the villain to your hero. Find the person who you are confident having in your corner, cheering you on while at the same time keeping you honest.

MEASURED HUMILITY

Take a moment to consider what you are asking of your strategist. This kind of person will inevitably be a highly skilled individual. It may be that they could pursue their own story and create their legacy. However, for some reason, they have decided to live in the credits of your movie. Without the humility needed to play second fiddle, they may eventually resent your success. Keep this in mind when deciding if they have the humility required to be content being the strategist to your futurist.

SHARED LEGACY

Ideally, find someone who can see what you see and be excited about seeing it become a reality. One of the great mistakes entrepreneurs make is being solely focused on leaving a legacy—for themselves. The larger your organisation becomes, the more team members you will likely employ. Have you considered that they, too, want to leave a legacy? Find your strategist among those of a similar tribe with a similar dream to make a similar impact on world history.

SHARING THE CREDITS

Give credit where credit is due. It has often been said that there would not be a Walt Disney Company without his brother Roy. If you are going to employ a yin to your yang, be careful to share both the legacy and the credits that go with success.

WORTHY REWARDS

When it comes to employing your strategist, don't be cheap. Early in a business's development, staff members are employed for their time. This is not so much the case when a company becomes larger, especially when it looks to take on legacy status. At this level of team acquisition, you are not paying so much for time but for perspective.

CHAPTER EIGHT

THE SIX SENSES OF LEADERSHIP

KEY POINTS

In this chapter, we explore a more intuitive leadership style aligned with our humanity's six senses. An intuitive leader can see the future, listen to stakeholders, smell when something is off, taste when something is on, touch lives with empathy, and have a sixth sense that foretells the next big thing.

Leaders are humans.

In a world of AI, one thing a computer cannot do—yet—is be human. Many years ago, I was invited to speak to teenagers on life skills and living with purpose. A few minutes into my presentation, I noticed one of the young girls get up and leave the room. Not long after, her friend rose and left. My heart sank as more teenagers walked out one by one until only a handful were left. By now, I'm feeling irritated. I'm beginning to feel offended at how rude these kids were for walking out on their invited speaker. I wasn't much older than my audience, probably in my early twenties, and I was somewhat angry. In hindsight, I was also a little immature for feeling that way.

After the meeting, the group organiser approached me and apologised for not informing me that one of the young people in the group had died in a car accident that afternoon.

Of course, that information changed everything. If I had known, the whole event would have been, at least, organised differently or cancelled. I was tone-deaf to the real atmosphere of the room. Why is this important? We are not machines that follow pre-set codes; we are human beings with emotions, compassion, empathy, and intellect.

We have the tall-poppy syndrome in New Zealand and Australia, where I have spent the entirety of my leadership journey. Instead of celebrating the success and promotion of our peers, there is a tendency to undermine them, pulling them back down to size. If anyone dares lift their head above the crowd, you can be sure someone out there will take a shot. At times like this, I feel like calling out, "Leaders are people, too".

This chapter digs a little deeper into that idea. Leaders are people. They are humans. They aren't machines who are tone-deaf to the emotions and experiences of those around us. We can align our leadership skills with our six natural senses in this context. We have sight, hearing, smell, taste, touch, and intuition. Each one brings a new insight into being a fully human leader.

THE SIX SENSES OF AN
INTUITIVE LEADER

ONE: SIGHT

They can see the future.

This book covers much about vision. It is likely the primary skill of a legacy leader. All leadership begins with an idea—a vision of the future. A legacy leader can see further into the future than others.

In my early twenties, I noticed headaches and difficulty focusing when reading. After a visit to an optometrist, I was diagnosed with long-sightedness. This means I have excellent eyesight when looking into the far distance, but things become blurry up close. Although this is a physical ailment, it perfectly describes my leadership style. I love thinking and dreaming about the future but get lost in too much up-close detail.

When the horse and cart dominated world transportation, Henry Ford's vision was to create an affordable automobile that could be manufactured at a lower cost without compromising quality. He believed every person should have access to transportation and transformed society by making cars accessible to ordinary people. His innovation led to the creation of the Model T, which fulfilled this vision and revolutionised the automotive industry.

Interestingly, his vision was likely a tiny part of the worldwide transformation motor vehicles would cause. All legacies begin with a long-sighted leader.

My advice is to practice being a leader with long-sightedness. I love to journal. As a daily practice, I ask the question, what do I need to see? In my mind, I paint a picture of my future life. What do I see in a year? What do I see in five years? What do I see when I retire? I break this question into areas of my life. What do

I see for my health, marriage, family, leisure, business, finance, investments, philanthropy, legacy, and holidays? Then, I gathered all my answers and wrote a future manifesto entitled The Future I See. I believe you will not live what you don't first see. Clarity of vision is the first step towards a lasting legacy.

TWO: HEARING

They listen to stakeholders.

Legacy leaders are great listeners. Many years ago, as a very young leader, I travelled with a mentor who often gave me advice and direction. I was likely being my usual arrogant, young self when he turned to me and told me I had become far too negative in my thinking. He added that being critical was not a good look.

My first reaction was to be defensive. Who does he think he is? I'm not negative! However, it was only a few seconds later that I came to my senses. I made a decision that would help me throughout the rest of my life. I chose to listen and change. I decided that I would do my best never to be a critic.

Listening goes beyond receiving constructive criticism and fully embraces listening to your stakeholders. How effectively you listen to your staff, customers, mentors, family, the market-place, and colleagues will profoundly affect whether you create a lasting legacy.

On April 23, 1985, Coca-Cola Company chairman and CEO Roberto Goizueta stepped before the press gathered at New York City's Lincoln Centre to introduce the new formula, which he declared to be "smoother, rounder, yet bolder—a more harmonious flavour." The press, however, said what Goizueta couldn't admit: New Coke tasted sweeter and more like Pepsi.

"Some may call this the boldest single marketing move in the history of the packaged goods business," Goizueta said. "We simply call it the surest move ever made."

Coca-Cola president Donald Keough echoed the certainty: "I've never been as confident about a decision as I am about the one we're announcing today."

Coca-Cola shares dropped on the New York Stock Exchange while its rivals rose. Pepsi gave its employees the day off and declared victory in full-page newspaper advertisements that boasted, "After 87 years of going at it eyeball to eyeball, the other guy just blinked."

New Coke left a bitter taste in the mouths of the company's loyal customers. Within weeks of the announcement, the company fielded 5,000 angry phone calls daily. By June, that number grew to 8,000 calls daily, a volume that forced the company to hire extra operators. "I don't think I'd be more upset if you were to burn the flag in our front yard," one disgruntled drinker wrote to company headquarters. At protests staged by grassroots groups such as "Old Cola Drinkers of America", consumers poured the contents of New Coke bottles into sewer drains. One Seattle consumer even filed suit against the company to force it to provide the old drink.

Seventy-nine days after their initial announcement, Coca-Cola executives once again held a press conference on July 11, 1985, to announce a mea culpa and the return of the original formula under the label "Coca-Cola Classic". "Our boss is the consumer," Keough said. "We want them to know we're really sorry." The news was so momentous that television networks broke into regular programming with special reports.

Coca-Cola Classic quickly outsold New Coke and, within a few months, had returned to its position as the top-selling cola, ahead of Pepsi.

We can learn much from this story. First, we can understand the consequences of not listening to our stakeholders before we make changes. Then, we can also learn from how quickly Coca-Cola acted when they did listen, and listen, they did.

Ask yourself, how do we listen to our stakeholders? The managing director of a building company I work with visits his display homes disguised as a customer and listens to potential buyers' comments. As he listens, he is already designing his next display homes, which will be released in three years' time.

Legacy leaders are great listeners.

THREE: SMELL

They can smell when something or someone is off.

Have you ever poured milk into your coffee only to find it lumpy and putrid? It may have been better to smell it first. Legacy leaders have an acute sense of smell and can quickly detect when something or someone smells off.

Several years ago, I worked with a successful leader, and a bright young applicant applied for a role within the organisation. On paper, he looked like a good match. He had the qualifications and the personality to be an asset to the team. Five minutes after meeting the young man, the business owner took me aside and said to reject the application. There was no explanation. The decision was made. No!

Did he have it right? Was he missing out on a potential star player? We will never know. All we know is he had a great sense of smell, and this guy didn't smell right. I did a follow-up to see where the young man landed. organisation employed him, and he did very well. However, I am also close with the other organisation and quickly surmised that he was much better suited to their environment. He wasn't a bad person; he was just wrong for this environment and right for another.

Having a keen sense of smell is a skill learned over time. Not everything that smells off is bad. Sometimes, things smell off because of our own psychological baggage. They smell off because they remind us of a previous negative experience.

It takes time to sift through the difference. And then there are times when good things don't smell right. Many years ago, while travelling and speaking in Malaysia, the locals were adamant I taste their local delicacy, durian. Durian is a local fruit that I was assured smelled like hell and tasted like heaven. They were half right. It did smell like hell!

The point is to learn to develop your sense of smell. When something or someone smells off, take note. Be bold enough to follow your gut and make the difficult calls to say no.

FOUR: TASTE

They can taste when something or someone is on.

One of the habits of great chefs is to taste the food before serving it to customers. Legacy leaders taste the broth before serving it to others.

In 2010, Australian billionaire Gerry Harvey donned a disguise and visited his successful Harvey Norman stores. Dressed as an older man, he undertook a taste test to experience customer service first-hand. He was not impressed. Having a television camera crew accompany him, he recorded the results under-cover. Shortly after the program aired, he and the television show were "swamped" with letters and emails complaining of poor service at the big retailer. Staff members exposed by the stunt for either poor service or the giving away of discounts were demanding an apology. However, changes were made.

Legacy leaders know their products and services. They undertake the taste test. Whether doing this themselves or continually receiving reviews and feedback, they ensure the soup tastes delicious before it hits the restaurant table.

Several years ago, I sat with a group of small business owners to help each one write an empathy map for their clients. We followed a fictitious new customer through their journey with the business. How did they first hear of the business? What was their first visit like? Could they easily find the address? How did they feel as they were travelling to the company? Could they find a car park? Upon entering, did they know where to go? Were they nervous? How were they welcomed? Did they need childcare? If they needed a health centre, did they know what to wear? Were there changing rooms available? Were people friendly? Did they know how to use the equipment?

Recently, I went for lunch at a newly opened local restaurant. We sat at the table, looked at the menu, and waited for a staff member to come and collect our order. After a long period of time, I went to the bar and suggested the waiting staff may have forgotten us. She looked at me strangely and suggested I should know that orders are taken at the bar. There was no table service. No apology. No empathy—just a good serving of humble pie.

It is so important to hone your sense of taste when building a legacy company. Create an empathy map and consider every-thing that could go wrong with your clients' experience. Taste the soup before it hits the restaurant table.

FIVE: TOUCH

They carry an empathy that serves and loves people.

Legacy leaders have a keen sense of touch. I am convinced that future opportunities will be in high-touch areas in a high-tech world. As already mentioned, we are all human beings. We crave community. Although systems and procedures are necessary to scale any business, we need to become smaller as we become larger.

In a 2014 tweet, Richard Branson wrote, "Train people well enough so they can leave. Treat them well enough so they don't want to." He is also quoted as saying, "Clients do not come first. Employees come first. If you take care of your employees, they will take care of the clients." Virgin has created over 300 branded companies worldwide, employing approximately 50,000 people in 30 countries. So, how does Virgin create a high-touch environment for such a large company? Branson has always strived to create a non-hierarchical, egalitarian, family-like culture in all his companies, where people like to work and come to work.

A recent Gallup newsletter noted that:

> *Psychological and psychosocial injury claims cost the Australian economy between A$12.2 billion and A$39.9 billion annually. Psychosocial hazards are the product of toxic workplace cultures and include factors such as lack of role clarity, unrealistic job demands, poor manager support, harmful colleague relationships, inadequate reward and recognition, and poor physical environments.*

We need to do better, and we can. The key is in how we define and implement culture. Being high-touch in a high-tech world is not something a leader can do alone. The larger an organisation grows, the less direct contact the senior leader will have with employees. Culture then becomes the defining factor. As our chapter on Culture Incarnate mentioned, culture comprises a group's shared beliefs, ideas, customs, language, actions, habits, and values. Consider the values that currently make up your culture and ask if the value of human kindness and dignity is included.

Many years ago, while in my mid-twenties, I worked in middle management at a large company. Late on a Friday afternoon, I was sadly informed of the death of my brother by suicide. Throughout the weekend, family and friends began to gather to offer sympathy and comfort. There was a work meeting planned for Sunday evening that I had no direct involvement in and had very little relevance to my role on the team. I called my boss, explained what was happening, and requested the evening off with family. The request was denied. In his view, loyalty to the workplace is rated higher than family. Being young and somewhat naïve, I complied. In hindsight, I regret not holding my ground. I would likely have been dismissed, but it would have been worth it to lock in my beliefs and values. The truth is people matter.

Legacy leaders will be better remembered if they are Hi-touch in a Hi-tech world.

SIX: INTUITION

They have a sixth sense that can foretell the next big thing.

Legacy leaders have a strong sense of intuition. We are considering this in the context of seeing the next big thing and being early adopters. When asked about intuition versus logic, Richard Branson said, "I rely far more on gut instincts than researching huge amounts of statistics." As he is often quoted, Branson believes that not everything can be summed up in a statistic and that intuition is the way to go to feel out the best path/result.

Steve Jobs said, "Don't let the noise of others drown your inner voice."

Malcolm Gladwell, in Blink: The Power of Thinking Without Thinking, describes how our initial split-second assessment of a situation often yields better results than months of belaboured "rational" research.

Albert Einstein is quoted as saying:

> *"The intuitive mind is a sacred gift, and the rational mind is a faithful servant. We have created a society that honours the servant and has forgotten the gift."*

How do we exercise our sense of intuition? I love the title of Richard Branson's autobiography, Screw It, Let's Do It. Perhaps unrelated to the book's content, it's a great picture of acting on intuition. There comes a time when you have completed the research and considered the pros and cons, and it's time for someone to make the call. You either walk away, or you step up and say, "Screw it, let's do it."

In 2001, I was invited to go on a speaking tour through Malaysia, Singapore, and the U.K. I decided it would be an excellent opportunity to take the family with me. Although it would cost around $20,000.00, it was an experience my children would be unlikely to have again in the foreseeable future. We were all looking forward to the adventure when, only a few months before our departure, 9/11 happened. The world was on high alert. Security at airports had been increased. There was an atmosphere of fear across the whole world.

We gathered with our leadership team and discussed whether it was wise to travel as a family in the current climate of fear and increased security. We talked for hours when one of our team members finally stood up and said, "You need to make a call. We are all waiting for faith to enter the room." She was right. I needed to dig deep, have some courage, and follow my intuition. This was a "Screw it, let's do it" moment. And that's what we did. It was a life-changing journey for our eight, ten, and eleven-year-old children. We even took a nanny with us so each child could have an adult accompanying them through security.

We will all have times when the data doesn't make the decision clear, and a leap of faith is required. In those times, we must listen to our deep inner voice and make the courageous call. Before we close on this thought, those calls based on intuition can also be when we need to say no. There have been countless times I have been pursuing a particular path or project when my intuition has been telling me to abandon it. I had chosen not to sign property contracts at the final step or abandon projects when my inner discomfort moved from a whisper to a shout.

How do we sharpen our intuition? I find my inner voice in the quietness of meditation. It is in the silence, without the noise of distraction, where my intuition speaks the loudest. I can be fully confident in public when I become fully convinced in private.

. . . . .

In closing out this chapter, I encourage you to be fully human in your leadership and let your senses guide you toward a legacy future.

PART TWO

EVERYTHING
IN BETWEEN

```
      ╭─────────╮                                    ╭─────────╮
     ╱           ╲        EVERYTHING                 ╱           ╲
    │  Seeing the │  •────────────────────▶         │ Making the │
    │   Unseen    │        IN BETWEEN                │  Unseen a  │
     ╲           ╱                                    │  Reality   │
      ╰─────────╯                                     ╲           ╱
                                                       ╰─────────╯
```

Part Two of The Legacy Leader is a collection of brief
lessons covering the "everything in between" of our
leadership model. Each Lesson is brief, to the point, and
full of wisdom gleaned from a forty-year
leadership journey.

LESSON ONE

LEADERS PLAY THE ORCHESTRA

Steve Jobs is quoted as saying, "Musicians play their instruments; I play the orchestra". One of the great challenges for entrepreneurs as their businesses grow is to put down their instruments and play the orchestra. Some refer to this as moving from hands-on to hands-off as a leader. Although this is mostly true, it is not an absolute rule.

You may have heard of James Dyson, the founder and chairman of the Dyson company and the inventor of the bagless vacuum cleaner. As his company grew, there is no doubt he played the orchestra and employed highly skilled executives. However, he also stayed intimately involved in research and development. Why? I suggest this is because he loves the inventive process. He could easily go hands-off but chose not to. He lived in the balance between playing the orchestra as a priority and maintaining and actively participating in the musical experience. Dyson currently has a research and development budget of half a billion pounds. This reflects the passion of its founder to both play the orchestra and drive his passion for invention.

The main point is this: There will come a time in your leadership journey when you must make a mind shift and transition from thinking like an employee to thinking like a leader. You will need to put down your tools and build your team. An old adage says, "I'd rather get ten people to do the work than do the work of ten people". Your first response to this statement may be that the person sharing it is lazy. Most times, however, it is simply a statement of wisdom. Consider it this way: some people would prefer to do the work of one person. They are satisfied with the results that one person can produce. However, legacy leaders tend to think of what could be achieved when a group of people collaborate so that the sum total of their collaborative efforts is greater than the total of their individual efforts. They love playing the orchestra.

I advise many of the leaders I work with to keep a record of their activities throughout the week and then ask what activities reflect playing in the orchestra and what activities reflect being the conductor. There is no right or wrong answer to this exercise. Some leaders love to play in the orchestra. However, the larger an orchestra grows, the more critical the role of the conductor becomes.

Throughout my leadership journey, large companies have asked me to help play their orchestra while the owner keeps his hand in playing the music. This is best practised when you grasp the concepts of the futurist and strategist working together in chapter seven. The futurist may be a freelance musician across the organisation, employing a strategist to lead and empower the team.

LEADERS ARE LEARNERS

"Graeme, I think you're stale," the elderly Irish Psychologist told me after one of our sessions. As I said earlier, I have developed a taste for humble pie over the years. I'm not going to pay the fee and not take the advice. In truth, he was right. It had been a harrowing few years, and I had neglected my commitment to learning in my efforts to keep my head above water. I have always been a learner. I love books, podcasts, and conferences. As I have grown older, I have been more selective about the well I choose to drink from, but learning is a priority.

I have created my own journaling system, where I ask five questions most days. The first of those questions is, "What do I need to learn?" I may read a chapter of a book or some scripture or listen to a podcast, then ask what I need to learn from this information. Perhaps, as a reader of this book, you have paused over a chapter or a page and asked, what do I need to learn from this idea? I have a friend who made a lifelong commitment to learning something new daily. He lived his life being curious.

Learning is acknowledging that what you know today may not be what you need to know to achieve your dreams tomorrow. When I stopped prioritising learning, I became stale. I was like a stagnant pond without fresh ideas and new concepts. It took a major shift in my circumstances to make a fresh start with new experiences and learning becoming a priority.

Learning has even greater benefits than only enhancing your leadership skills. Research has shown that learning in later life protects the brain against ageing and promotes 'neuroplasticity' (the brain's ability to develop new neural pathways). Professor Ross Cunnington from the University of Queensland, Australia, made this observation:

> You cannot learn something without storing it in some form of memory for future use. From neuroscience, we know that physical changes in the brain encode memories. In other words, your brain changes physically whenever you learn anything, and your brain continues to be moulded by experience and learning throughout your life.

Commit today to a life of learning.

Finally, here are my five daily questions:

1. What do I need to learn?

2. What do I need to see?

3. What do I need to say?

4. What do I need to do?

5. What do I need to expect?

LEADERS ARE LIKEABLE

Every time he walked into the room, the social temperature rose. People enjoyed being in his presence. He was fun, positive, and cool. He had a way of making you feel important when he spoke with you. This was the feeling I had when spending time with one of the most influential leaders I have ever met. His organisation grew into one of the largest of its kind in the world.

Not every legacy leader is likeable, but it certainly helps. It has been said that people don't resign and leave their jobs, but their managers. How likeable are you? Are you kind? Are you interested in others? Do you keep your cool when under pressure? Do you take time to talk to those on the shop floor? Likeability is an essential leadership attribute.

There is, however, a difference between being likeable and being liked by everyone. If your goal is to be liked by everyone, you will lose your credibility as a leader. Leaders make decisions, and not everyone will like those decisions. There are often winners and losers. Those who lose on account of your decisions may not like you. That is the burden every leader carries. At best, our goal is to be the most likeable person we can be while being disliked by many.

I have met thousands of leaders in my lifetime, and the irony is that some of the most disliked leaders worldwide are also the most likeable. If I were to give you the leader's name in my opening paragraph, and you were to type his name into Google, you would find both immense praise and extreme hate.

So, how do we approach this subject of being likeable? Consider these four thoughts to guide you:

- Just be nice. You don't need a PhD to learn how. The golden rule will suffice. Treat others the same way you would like to be treated.

- Just because you aspire to be likeable, don't expect everyone to like you. The higher you rise as a leader, the greater the target you become. If you are likeable, and others dislike you, it says more about them than you. Far worse to be disliked because you are an ass!

- The first person who needs to like you is you. How can you expect anyone else to like you if you don't? Jesus called his followers to love their neighbour as they loved themselves. If you don't love yourself, how can you love your neighbour?

- The greatest legacy you can leave is for your children to like you. That's as good a place as any to start.

LEADERS ARE TRAINED OPTIMISTS

Have you ever been asked whether you are a glass-half-empty or glass-half-full person? My response is that the glass is always full. It is full of water and air, but always full. In truth, I am a born pessimist but a trained optimist. My natural tendency is negativity. I have, at times, battled with depression and worked hard to believe that the light at the end of the tunnel is not a train coming my way. I have decided that as a leader, those around me need me to be a beacon of hope.

This doesn't mean I am not a realist. I am the first to present the facts. If we don't know the problems, we will never be able to solve them. However, I refuse to entertain the idea that a problem is terminal. I have decided to be an optimist. There is no negotiation on that decision. There is always a solution; if we are not ahead on the board, the race is not yet over.

Only once in my career have I lost all hope. I have already written about a season in our lives when we changed everything. We resigned from our roles, sold our home, and started new careers. We felt like we were in a chess game, and our opponent had us in checkmate. Being in checkmate can easily be construed as failure. But this is only the case if you also believe that chess is the only game in town. A pessimist will believe that checkmate means the game is over. A trained optimist will think they may be better at different games: checkers, golf, or clay shooting.

In my view, optimism is a discipline. It is a firm decision to be a dispenser of hope. Optimistic leaders instil hope, inspire confidence, and create a positive environment despite adversity. Their belief in positive outcomes and better tomorrows drives their teams to persevere, innovate, and take calculated risks.

Perhaps one of the best examples of optimism is that of Winston Churchill, who faced almost inevitable defeat at the hands of Hitler's advancing armies. Live on air, he spoke to the nation, including these words:

> "We shall fight in France, we shall fight on the seas and oceans, we shall fight with growing confidence and growing strength in the air, we shall defend our island, whatever the cost may be. We shall fight on the beaches, we shall fight on the landing grounds, we shall fight in the fields and in the streets, we shall fight in the hills; we shall never surrender."

Ask yourself the question, are you a trained optimist? With discipline, can you find the silver lining with every cloud? Are you the voice of hope and positivity in every crisis? Of course, optimism should only be dispensed with great wisdom. There is a time to weep with those who weep and grieve with those who grieve but, in general terms, choose to err on the side of hope.

LEADERS ARE ACCOUNTABLE

Autocracy is a form of governance in which one person has absolute power. Of course, the opposite of autocracy is a democracy, a form of government by the people, often through elected members or majority rule. Neither works well in the world of business.

Many business owners face the challenge of transitioning from autocratic leadership to some level of accountability. They began their businesses as sole traders. It was self-rule, self-motivation, and self-discipline. They became successful by taking responsibility for every aspect of the operation. If it's going to be, it's up to me. This may be acceptable in the early days, but not so much when you have a team. Let me be honest, you cannot be trusted with absolute power. Lord Acton, a 19th-century British politician, said, "Power tends to corrupt, and absolute power corrupts absolutely."

Accountability is a decision to yield your independence voluntarily. You may not have to. You may say, "Nobody gets to tell me what to do." If this is your belief, you may be gifted but also stupid. I believe legacy leaders allow themselves to be accountable for their actions as they lead others towards a better and more secure future, often at the expense of their freedom or comfort. Bad leaders refuse accountability as they lead themselves towards a better and more secure future, often at the expense of others.

Consider the following four accountability relationships you need in your world.

Personal accountability.

Is there anyone you have permitted to ask you the hard questions? What do you view on the internet, whether you are being faithful to your spouse or maintaining proper boundaries concerning alcohol, gambling, financial integrity, or healthy routines? Of course, one final question could be, have you just lied to me?

Business accountability.

Is there anyone more intelligent than you to whom you seek counsel concerning business decisions? Do you have a business coach or mentor to whom you listen?

Financial accountability.

Who looks over your books? Do you have an accountant? Are your books audited? Have you eliminated the option to be dishonest or lack financial integrity?

Project accountability.

Is there a culture of accountability throughout your team where projects are broken down into tasks with someone responsible for meeting deadlines?

Make accountability a cultural norm across every leadership and staff level throughout your organisation.

LEADERS THINK GENERATIONALLY

This leadership lesson is at the very heart of being a legacy leader. If the definition of legacy is "what we leave behind" and "what we will be remembered for", thinking generationally is our primary worldview.

Walther de Gray, the Archbishop of York, began building the great Gothic-style Cathedral of York in 1215. It was finally declared complete and consecrated in 1472, two hundred and fifty-seven years later. Walter de Gray died in 1255, forty years into the building process and two hundred and seventeen years before completion. Imagine being a stonemason working your entire career as a skilled artisan on the great cathedral, knowing you would never see it finished. It would not be finished for another two centuries after you retired. Imagine being the architect, designing a cathedral you would never see complete. And yet, if you were to travel to York in North Yorkshire, England, today, you could experience the sense of awe that is the legacy of Walter de Gray.

Thinking generationally is often a mind shift that becomes more pronounced as we age. Early in life, we tend to be ambitious about "making our mark" and achieving greatness for ourselves. However, as we become wiser, we understand that we are only passing through. An ancient text says, "For what is your life? It is even a vapour that appears for a little time and then vanishes away." (James 4:14). What truly matters is not how much money we accumulate or toys we have acquired but whether we did good and left the world better than we found it.

Consider the following five options for thinking generationally:

1. Start with family. If you have been blessed with children, they are your greatest opportunity to build a legacy. Their inheritance is not only what you leave them but who they become. Commit today to making your family your priority.

2. Choose to be a positive influence on everyone you meet. We live in a world craving encouragement. It costs you nothing but a little time to encourage even a stranger along the way.

3. Be content in the credits of other people's movies. You don't need to be the star of every show. Helping others succeed is often where we find our own success.

4. Think generationally when building your business or organisation. How can you set the next generation up for success as they build on your foundations? They will be able to see much further by standing on your shoulders.

5. Write it down. Whatever processes within your business or wisdom you have gathered along the way. Write it down for others to benefit from after you're gone.

LEADERS EAT THE FROG

Procrastination is often the weakness of many leaders. "Eat the frog" is a saying that motivational speaker Brian Tracy coined. It means completing difficult, frustrating, or tedious tasks—also known as frogs—before the ones you'd rather do, getting them over with. Tracy's best-selling book from 2001, Eat That Frog! explores this task prioritisation strategy.

We all have our frogs. What may be a frog to you may be a delicacy to others. I don't enjoy making appointments with people. I'd much prefer to automate appointments with an app like Calendly. However, there are times when I need to eat the frog. As I write today, I am reminded of a phone call I have been putting off for weeks. I'll be right back!

Okay, call made, and frog eaten!

Consider making the following five commitments to help you eat the frog:

1. *Do it now and do it fast.*

If you know it needs to be done but don't want to, do it now and do it fast. Don't linger, don't look for excuses, get it done now. Book the dentist appointment. Apologise to your spouse or partner. Make the call to an underperforming team member. Do it now, do it fast, and enjoy the rest of your day.

2. *Make it a habit.*

James Clear wrote in his book Atomic Habits, "You do not rise to the level of your goals. You fall to the level of your systems." Consider beginning your day with eating the frogs. Get them out of the way and set yourself up for greater productivity.

3. *Plan the night before.*

Sometimes, when we wake up at night, our minds can be busy thinking about our uneaten frogs. If it's on the calendar for the morning, we can rest easy knowing that the decision has been made and that it is on our agenda for tomorrow.

4. *What to do with multiple frogs.*

If you have multiple frogs, choose the one that will create the biggest win first. It may not be the biggest and ugliest, but it will give you the most immense sense of satisfaction.

5. *Add some seasoning.*

Sometimes, we can make the experience more pleasant to the taste. For example, sometimes I work better with a team. If I have a bunch of calls to make, I may bring in a team member and tackle them together. Alternatively, I will brew my favourite coffee, put some jazz on my turntable, and tackle a task I have been avoiding.

LEADERS EMPLOY FROG-EATERS

Let's face it, frogs are not very appetising. And what's more, some people like eating frogs much more than you do. For this reason, I suggest employing frog eaters. The point is, for them, they are not frogs. They are a delicacy.

There will be some activities that you are not good at, and to be honest, you may never be good at. For example, you may never be good at writing employment contracts. That is not to say you can't learn how to do it, but you will never enjoy it. There is good news. There are people out there who love writing employment contracts. Your frog is their caviar. Hire them.

One piece of advice Richard Branson gives young entrepreneurs is to learn to delegate. He believes he would never have been able to build his business had he not learnt to delegate early on.

Sometimes, you will need to be creative in your employment decisions. Fractional work is becoming more common in modern times. For example, you may not be ready to hire a CFO, but you may be able to source a virtual CFO on a fractional arrangement. One of my clients has seen phenomenal growth over only a few years. A virtual CFO provided him with a monthly financial dashboard that gave a clear picture of cash flow, gross and net profit, overheads, and profit margins specific to both products and branches at a fraction of the price of a full-time role. He purchased peace of mind and better sleep at night by employing a frog-eater.

Consider these three keys to hiring frog eaters:

1. *Identify your strengths and weaknesses.*

You can do this by using online surveys like the Clifton Strengthsfinder Assessment, asking family and friends, or being honest with yourself. You can then double down on your strengths and hire for your weaknesses.

2. *Identify what's missing.*

Not only do you have strengths and weaknesses, but so does your business or organisation. You can get some clarity by undertaking a SWOT analysis. Many people will be available to help you with this. Once you have the results, develop a strategy to fill the gaps and help you build your dream team.

3. *Open your boardroom door.*

You may be amazed at how much information you can glean from your team if you listen. Many larger organisations are divided between the board room and the shop floor. The boardroom is often referred to as "they". What are "they" doing this time? "They" don't understand what it's like. If only "they" would listen. "They" don't care. Find ways of listening to all your team members. Remain visible, approachable, and connected to all the moving parts of your business. You will soon hear of the uneaten frogs.

LEADERS ASK THE RIGHT QUESTIONS

One of the mistakes many leaders make is assuming their teams are looking to them for answers. They believe that bold confidence and grand statements will build people's confidence in their competence, but research has shown that the opposite is true. Believing and behaving like you have all the answers erodes trust. In a rapidly changing and uncertain world, being vulnerable and asking questions demonstrates your trust in others and encourages trust in return. People know you don't have all the answers. No one does. So, by not asking questions, you are demonstrating arrogance, not competence.

I often meet with young aspiring leaders for group mentoring and coaching. Most of the time, there is a know-it-all in the group. They don't ask questions. Their default is to solve the problems of others with their superior knowledge and experience. Their hope for respect and admiration is in vain. I soon learnt to make a rule in our gatherings. No one was allowed to offer advice to another member's problem. They were only allowed to share an experience they had been through, their approach, and the outcome of their actions.

Intelligent leaders ask powerful and inspiring questions that convey that they don't have all the answers but are willing to invite others into the conversation. We should ask upwards, sideways, and beneath. Upwards are those in leadership or mentors who have travelled further than us. Sideways are our colleagues and co-workers who have insights that complement our own. Downwards are those on our teams who have valuable insights and will feel part of the team if their voice is heard.

Consider some of these questions that could help you go to a new level of productivity if you began to ask:

- What is a game-changing opportunity that could create more value than we have delivered in the past?

- What is the greatest need of our ideal client?

- What could we change that would increase our employees' enjoyment at work and contribute to their work-life balance?

- What new technology has the potential to disrupt our industry?

- What are our competitors doing that could threaten our position in the market?

- What skill set is currently missing from our organisation that would make the most significant difference if we filled it?

Finally, if you will ask questions, ask smart questions, not stupid ones. There are some things you should know. Asking the right questions creates a culture of curiosity. You encourage your entire team to ask the right questions. The result will be a fresh and innovative company.

LEADERS ARE NETWORKERS

Almost every new opportunity I have experienced has come through networking. Have you ever said, "I can't help you, but I know someone who can"? You may be surprised how often that statement is made. You need to be the "someone who can". If I need a fence built on my property, and I see my neighbour has recently had a new one built, you can be sure I will ask who he used. Referrals will always be your best source of new opportunities.

Admittedly, I have only needed to look for employment a few times in my career—perhaps half a dozen—but rarely have I found employment through the normal interview process. Most times, someone I knew "knew a guy", and that guy was me. Networking will open new doors, expand horizons, and provide access to knowledge and opportunities. It will also allow you to refer others, giving them opportunities they would not have access to if they didn't know you. In this way, networking is intentionally building mutually beneficial relationships.

When we changed careers in 2010, I knew a guy in Adelaide, Australia, who could help us with counselling. He knew a guy in Melbourne who needed someone like me to fill a twelve-month leadership role. In the Melbourne organisation, I met a guy who knew a guy who needed someone for a two-year contract in leadership. In that role, I met a guy who needed someone to set up leadership and business coaching in a growing business community. In that role, I met a guy with a brother-in-law who needed someone to consult about the leadership and structure of his growing company. In that role, another large national company in Australia heard of the impact I was making and asked me to do the same for his company.

Networking could be the missing link in your next big opportunity. Here are a few pointers:

Be genuine.

Show genuine interest in others and foster relationships based on mutual respect.

Turn up.

You may not feel like a networking event on a cold winter morning, but turning up is the first step towards new opportunities.

Offer value.

Don't look for referrals. Offer referrals. It is often in helping others that we find our own success. One of your most powerful statements is, "How can I help?"

Follow up.

When you meet someone with whom you share a connection, follow up. Send an email of appreciation. If they share a challenge they are going through, follow up and see how they went. Networking should be wide and deep.

LEADERS EXERCISE SELF-CARE

You may have heard, "You cannot pour from an empty cup." This is one of my greatest lessons. If I were to list my regrets, this one would be high. A healthy me is one of, if not the most valuable, gifts I can give my family, co-workers, and customers. At my best, I am a valued commodity. I cannot offer my best when unwell, anxious, or burnt out.

Professional athletes treat training and recovery as two sides of their performance coin. They are as serious about their recovery as they are about their training. I consider this principle to be the rhythm of high performance. Preparation, performance, replenishment, repeat.

We could divide self-care into several categories: physical, emotional, mental, social, and personal. However, this is a brief lesson, not a book. Instead, we will ask: What do you need to do today that will contribute to a healthier you? The longer you live, the easier you can answer this question. For example, for fifteen years, I was based in Dunedin, a university city in the south of New Zealand. Queenstown is a magnificent tourist destination approximately three hours' drive away. My wife and I would take a few days off every few months, book a hotel in Queenstown, and recharge our batteries. If we were to neglect this routine, I would lose my edge. I knew when my emotional tanks were empty and what refuelled them. Knowing what contributes to your recovery enables you to create your self-care routines.

Now, living in Australia, at the top of my list of self-care goals is to "find my Queenstown." Where do I best recharge? What is your best current investment regarding self-care? Where do you replenish? What have you let go?

Here is a list you can choose from to get you started:

Physical health.

Am I overweight? Do I sleep well? Am I moving? What am I eating?

Emotional health.

How do I manage my stress levels? Do I know what replenishes me emotionally? Do I take time for personal reflection? Do I prioritise time for myself?

Mental health.

Do I know when and how to switch off? Do I manage my calendar to include breaks? What do I enjoy doing? What makes me happy? When did I last immerse myself in an activity separate from my work?

Social health.

Do I have replenishing and draining relationships? Do I balance both? Do I prioritise friends and family?

Personal health.

How is my "me time"? Do I practice gratitude daily? Do I have a solitude routine?

LEADERS ARE FINANCIALLY LITERATE

Being financially literate is one of the most valuable tools in a leader's arsenal. There are no hard and fast rules regarding how literate you need to be, but there are some basics you need to get right. For example, Richard Branson said his first hire was an accountant. You can delegate as much as you need to, and a good bookkeeper, accountant, and CFO will be beneficial, if not necessary, but you will still need a level of literacy.

I have met many business leaders who are still unsure about terms such as gross and net profit, break-even, cost of sale, margins, cash flow, or how to read a balance sheet accurately. For the sake of this brief lesson, what do you need to know? Consider the following as a brief introduction:

1. *Pricing*

Pricing is a good starting point for your financial literacy journey. At first glance, it may appear simple. I bought a pencil for a dollar and am selling it for two dollars. However, there are a myriad of other questions that will make up the equation. What about your overheads? Transport, storage, electricity, staff, and your own time. Is the pencil worth two dollars? How much are your competitors selling pencils for? How many pencils will you need to sell for you to make a tidy profit?

2. *Break-even*

Break-even is the number of pencils you sell before seeing a net profit. For example, a thousand pencils would pay the purchase price of a thousand dollars plus a thousand dollars in gross profit. But you are still losing money if you rent a facility for a thousand dollars a week and have a part-time bookkeeper, electricity costs, and office expenses. You haven't even paid yourself yet. Knowing your break-even number is a must.

3. *Cashflow*

This may also seem quite simple. My costs are a set amount, and as long as my income exceeds that number, I'm in profit. But it's more complex. How much money will you lose before you break even? How much start-up money will you need? Can you sell the pencils before you pay for their purchase? If not, what is the gap between paying for the pencils and finally selling them? Can you survive that gap?

We are only scratching the surface in this brief lesson. Still, the point is this: You need both a broad understanding of finance principles and enough financial literacy to read the numbers and act appropriately. The big picture is that you need more money coming in than going out. The details are then about ensuring we are literate enough to understand the reports.

LEADERS CREATE ATMOSPHERES

Do you know that everyone carries an atmosphere?

Many years ago, I led an organisation with several interns who were training for future leadership. I noticed that some interns were attending meetings with a demeanour of sadness and negativity. From an outward perspective, they presented themselves as if it was the last place they wanted to be. One, with long flowing hair, would sit in the meetings, hiding behind her hair with her head down. Others were barely human before their second coffee. We checked in on their mental health and found everyone was okay and that they presented as warm and sociable in other situations. They didn't like being an intern. However, it was a necessary part of their college studies, and they wanted to graduate.

Eventually, we called them together to address the issue. We discussed how leaders create atmospheres and how they can change them when entering a room. Like a thermostat, they can lift the room's mood with hope and positivity during difficult times or bring a sense of focus and stability in chaos and disorganisation. Perhaps I was young and inexperienced, or it may have been a culture clash of a boomer speaking to millennials, but my following words created an adverse reaction I was not expecting.

I suggested they read the mood of a room and, as a leader, reflect the mood they were looking for, not their current internal feelings. All hell broke loose! The common response was, "I will not fake my feelings." or "I can't be happy externally if I am sad internally." as well as "You are wrong to expect otherwise."

This presents a question that, as a leader, you will inevitably face. Were they right? Should we fake it? I remember one of my leaders in the 1980s telling people to get a check-up from the neck-up and to quit their stinking thinking! I have even heard a leader suggest people drink wet concrete and harden up.

The answer is not as simple as it may appear. Our challenge is to live in the tension between vulnerability and positivity. The first answer is, "Yes, they were right. We shouldn't fake it. If we are in crisis, we need the vulnerability to accept the support and encouragement we need". The second answer is, "No, they were wrong. If you have a negative attitude and cannot read the room and lift the mood, there is little hope of being an inspiring leader."

I think this: Everything has a time and place. There is a time to weep, a time to laugh, a time to mourn, and a time to celebrate. It's about time and place. We can weep and mourn when appropriate, but being a leader means we are responsible for reading the room and changing the atmosphere.

A few years after this experience, one of the interns visited me to apologise. He made an insightful statement. "We were there to study knowledge; you were there to make leaders of us." It was a conflict of purpose.

LEADERS LEVERAGE

In my previous book, Life Change, I dedicated a chapter to leverage, "Leverage Everything." In the chapter, I shared my experience of resetting my phone. Frustrated that my phone was not working, I pressed factory reset. This was before phones could be backed up to the cloud.

When my phone slowly returned to life, I found I had lost all my data—contacts, memos, and photos. I was devastated. I would have to start again. All the valuable relationships I had garnered over the years and their contact information were gone. The lesson is this: You have many contacts and experiences you can draw upon in your leadership journey. You are not beginning each day with a factory reset. Leverage everything.

In my season of greatest crisis, leverage was the key to my eventual success. Moving from almost thirty years in the not-for-profit sector as an ordained minister into the business sector has immense challenges. What could I offer to the business community? I was forty-eight years old and felt like I was starting again. But was I? Not at all. Here is a list of what I had available to me to leverage my way into a new career:

Experience and qualifications.

Many years ago, I began a business degree I had never completed. Knowing I would need leverage for future opportunities, I returned to complete a Bachelor of Applied Management with a double major in entrepreneurship and strategic management. I also used my experience in public speaking, writing, counselling, leadership development, and community service as transferable skills to open new doors of opportunity. Leverage everything.

Friends and acquaintances.

People are often our significant resource. As leaders, we can often ask, "Who can help me?" Who can introduce me to the right people? Who can I ask for advice? Who might give me a reference? You may feel uncomfortable using friends as leverage, but friends often exist for such times. They want to help you and are waiting for you to ask. Leverage everything.

Resources.

One of my greatest strengths and weaknesses is that I live with a deep sense of purpose. When taking risks, I am often ready to leverage my resources. I have sold homes, hobbies, and treasures to finance the dream. This has been a weakness when I have put purpose before family, but a strength when we have sacrificed material resources for the greater dream together.

Leverage is your friend. When you are in a crisis or challenge, ask what experience you can draw from. Who can you ask for help? What resources can you leverage to achieve the greater good?

LESSON FIFTEEN

LEADERS ARE PERSUASIVE

In chapter one, we said that leadership gets things done, creates more opportunities, influences more lives, makes more money, and leaves greater legacies. Getting things done implies utilising the skills and efforts of others. The idea that we would prefer to get ten people to do the work than do the work of ten people also implies utilising the skills and efforts of others.

So, how do we convince others to do the work? Some may say through personal reward. We pay people to do stuff that we need to get done. However, that leaves us at the mercy of someone willing to pay them more. For many years, I was involved in the not-for-profit sector, which often meant utilising the time and effort of volunteers. Financial rewards were not an option for motivation. This left two options: persuasion or manipulation. Unfortunately, I have seen too many examples of manipulation.

Manipulation usually involves coercion, guilt, or the use of authoritative power. Persuasion, on the other hand, is about building trust, credibility, and influence. To be an effective leader, we need to master the art of persuasion from a place of generosity rather than personal gain. If we get others to do stuff for personal gain, even our persuasion is only manipulating people dressed in different clothes. It is the classic wolf in sheep's clothing. Consider the following principles of persuasion:

Identify the shared cause.

People will make sacrifices for a common cause, and if they share your cause, they will go the extra mile.

Move from communication to connection.

Everyone communicates, but not all connect. Connection is moving beyond the use of language to becoming inclusive and empathetic. Invite people to join your tribe.

Build trust.

Trust is the currency of leadership. If your employees or team don't trust you, they will not follow you. They are little more than servants. Trust takes time, transparency, honesty, and consistency. Do the right thing over time, and trust will become your friend.

Be inspirational.

Practice your ability to inspire and motivate others. Paint a picture of a compelling future, clearly showing the benefits and opportunities that will come as we reach our goals. Invite your team to become part of something bigger than themselves.

Set, communicate, and achieve goals.

Set the goal, and then celebrate the milestones. If a lofty goal is never met, it only breeds disappointment. Celebrate your small successes and share the credit.

LESSON SIXTEEN

LEADERS ARE DECISIVE

In our chapter, Leaders are Likeable; we commented that being likeable doesn't equate with everyone liking you. The reason for this is primarily linked to decision-making. You can be the nicest person on earth, but you will not be liked if your decision harms one or more people. Historically, they crucified the nicest guy on the planet! I have seen many leaders become paralysed around a decision because they didn't want to offend a stakeholder. The outcome of this level of paralysis is living to the lowest common denominator. You will never build a legacy business by pleasing everyone.

Legacy leaders are decisive. For this reason, you will need to choose which of the four approaches to decision-making you adhere to. Here they are:

Autocratic Decision Making: The King Rules.

Of course, this is the most efficient style of decision-making. One person makes the decision. There are times when this is necessary, but it is rarely the best choice. My advice is to use this approach only in emergencies.

Democratic Decision Making: The Majority Rules.

Whole nations choose this type of leadership. The idea with the most votes wins. The problem with this style is that most voting people don't have enough skin in the game. Why would a business owner risk their life savings on a decision where they were outvoted? If a business fails, most employees will apply for a new job and be back on track in several weeks. However, the owner is in bankruptcy court and potentially has their house repossessed. Only use this approach when the stakes are low.

Consensual Decision Making: 100% agreement.

With this approach, we won't do it unless everyone agrees. This is more common in partnerships and family-owned businesses. 100% agreement is a worthy aim, but it can stalemate the business. Sometimes, any decision is better than no decision at all.

Collaborative Decision Making: Single Decision-maker who invites input.

Collaborative decision-making is like the autocratic approach, but the leader first invites experts and stakeholders to influence and shape the decision. Most businesses with a sole owner operate this way, which is, in my view, the most effective way. The goal is to genuinely take and consider the input of others and then make a decision with wisdom and empathy.

The key to being decisive as a leader is knowing when to act. As often as possible, take your time to gather and analyse the data, but to dare to leap when the time is right. Procrastination is the enemy of the decisive leader.

LESSON SEVENTEEN

LEADERS CREATE A COMMUNITY

Workplaces are, in essence, communities. A sense of community or camaraderie is consistently rated high in surveys measuring the critical attributes of an ideal workplace. With the time and effort most people put into their work, it is only reasonable that they should expect their workplace to be a meaningful, supportive, and healthy community. Of course, not every leader can be a social butterfly. Many leaders are introverts, and the last thing they desire is to be the centre of attention at the office party. However, I would suggest two ways a community is created in the workplace: by default or design.

If we leave a sense of community to be created by default, the loudest voice in the room will prevail. The community will be created, but it may or may not be healthy. Depending on the loudest voice, it may be tainted with bullying, demeaning others, and sarcasm or, alternatively, warm, healthy, and affirming.

A better option is to be intentional and create a sense of community by design. Consider the following keys to creating community by design:

If it's not your strength, delegate.

Creating a community can be the responsibility of an HR employee or, in a small business, a personable staff member. The key is to ask for help. Find someone to organise regular social events and help create a safe workplace.

Have a staff handbook as part of your onboarding documentation.

Most larger companies provide new employees with a staff handbook outlining company policies and guidelines. Ensure your policies include workplace culture, bullying, and any form of discrimination or antisocial behaviour.

Walk through the room slowly.

Slow down and talk to people. Most entrepreneurs tend to be more task-focused than people-focused. When did you last ask an employee about their weekend, family, or plans? It only takes a little time to be kind.

Ask for input.

People feel valued when their input is valued. Take the time to ask even your newest employee for advice. Let them contribute to the vision and culture, and thank them for their contribution.

Remember names.

This has always been a challenge for me. The larger the organisation I work with, the more challenging it becomes to remember names. However, most people feel more connected if we remember and address them by name. It makes a difference. They will feel even more valuable if you remember the names of their family members.

Be interested.

Ask about family members and follow up on information shared. Returning and asking how "Johny did at the school cross-country" or "how their elderly parents recover after illness" will turn a workplace into a family.

LEADERS CELEBRATE TEAM WINS

No one runs a race without a finish line. Workplaces without milestones and wins can become monotonous and even soul-destroying. Celebrating team wins will boost morale, foster a positive environment, and inspire a team to strive for excellence. The recruiting site Indeed has shown that the No. 4 reason that someone may quit a job is due to feelings of being undervalued, and the No. 7 reason is that they require more feedback or structure. In our chapter about metamodernists, we observed that emerging generations continually seek feedback and affirmation. We can contribute to this need by celebrating team and individual wins.

In my experience, celebrating wins has significant advantages in the workplace, contributing to increased motivation, affirmation, recognition, community, variety, focus, inspiration, and engagement. This is an excellent return on a seemingly small investment. Let's quickly address each one:

Motivation

Nothing breeds success like success. Celebrating a win motivates a team to win again. What we celebrate will soon be recognised as valuable within the company and worth pursuing again.

Affirmation

You may be surprised how many people seek affirmation. Being recognised for making a positive contribution can do wonders for their self-esteem. In a world of cynicism and negativity, we can build others up by celebrating their presence on our team.

Recognition

Recognition gives people an opportunity to prove their critics wrong. Imagine being told you will never amount to anything and then being recognised for success. Surely, this is what legacy leadership is all about.

Community

Have you ever been part of a winning team on a sports field? Have you ever been in the changing room after a game singing your team song? I still remember celebrating with my school hockey team almost half a century ago. I was part of something great. It was good to feel like I belonged.

Variety

Celebrating wins breaks the monotony. It allows everyone to put their tools down and celebrate. Working without celebrating wins is like a room without windows.

Focus

Celebrating wins reminds us of why we do what we do. It brings the vision back to our attention. This is why we do what we do.

Inspiration

Even acknowledging small wins inspires people. There is nothing quite like a "thank you" or "well done" to lift someone's spirits.

Engagement

One of the significant challenges of any workplace is keeping employees engaged. Celebrating with their leaders and managers brings a team together and connects them with the cause.

With so many benefits and rewards, take some time to consider how you can begin to celebrate the wins within your organisation.

LEADERS BUILD ROADMAPS

One of the most important contributions I can make to the leaders I work with is helping them build roadmaps for the future. By creating a roadmap, I have witnessed companies achieve significantly more in one year than in the previous three to five years. One of my privileges is working with my son Daniel to mentor and coach business owners. One of our key offerings is meeting with teams and creating a yearly strategic plan as a live document, continually updated as milestones are reached. It has strategic plans, tasks, due dates, and accountability. It brings focus, efficiency, and productivity that some businesses have never experienced. The results are outstanding.

As a leader, you create roadmaps your teams can follow to achieve great results. In very general terms, I follow a principle I have coined: R.A.P.—Reality, Aspiration, and Process:

Reality

What is the current reality? You won't know where you are starting until you have an accurate picture of your current reality. When I lived in New Zealand, every six months, the law required me to take my car in for a warrant of fitness. A mechanic would check over the vehicle and, without fixing anything, write a list of what is needed to make it road-worthy. The faults would need rectified, and the vehicle would need to pass another test before it could be driven on the road again.

Your business or organisation needs an annual warrant of fitness. A SWOT analysis is often used to identify the current reality, or you can bring in an independent mentor or consultant.

Aspiration

What is your aspiration? Knowing your current reality, what would you like your destination to be? If you had to choose three issues you would like resolved in the next twelve months, what would they be? Describe what your organisation would look like at its best. How would your team feel if these improvements were made?

Process

Build the roadmap. What process will you create to get you from your current reality to your preferred aspiration? Make the plan as detailed as possible. For each core issue, write a list of tasks or milestones. Besides each task, write a completion date and a person responsible for making it happen. Using a spreadsheet, have a column where each task is red until it is started. When it is underway, change the red to yellow. When it is complete, change the yellow to green.

Feel free to get in touch if you need help building your roadmap.

LESSON TWENTY

LEADERS KEEP PROMISES

This is such an important principle. Leaders keep their promises, or at the very least, when promises are broken, they apologise and renegotiate. A good reputation can take years to build and moments to destroy. I have mentioned earlier that the currency of leadership is trust. Trust is like a bank account. The "trust" account begins relatively empty when a new employee joins your team. It may be in credit because of your brand or reputation in the industry or overdraft because of a negative experience the employee may have had in their previous workplace. Over time, team members gain confidence and deposit more trust in the account.

The time will come when you make a withdrawal. Perhaps you ask them to stay late to finish a project or go the extra mile during a busy time. If you reward them with a note or thanks, offer them time off in lieu, or show your appreciation in some meaningful way, they will redeposit the trust you withdrew from the account with interest added. The key is to recognise your trust in the bank account with each employee and make withdrawals commensurate with the balance available.

Here is the point of this lesson. Break a promise, and the balance is gone. Break another promise, and you will be in overdraft. Your employee is now operating from a position of distrust. Break too many promises, and you become bankrupt. That employee will be working for your competitors.

So, how do leaders keep their promises?

Don't make promises.

The easiest way to keep promises is not to make them in the first place. Most times, they are unnecessary. A better option is to share your hopes and intentions. If things go well, we hope to do this. However, this would require two outcomes. First, you need things to go well; otherwise, the intention never comes to pass. Second, when things go well, do what you said you hoped to do.

Don't forget your promises.

You may not have meant your words to be a promise, but they might have been received that way. How often have you reassured a team member that you would follow up on a conversation with them next week or that you would return to them by the end of the month, only to forget? On your part, it may only be a memory issue, but to your team members, it is a matter of trust.

Find out what promises you inherit when taking on a new role.

You may not have made the promise, but you must know if the previous leader did. You may deliver on it or renegotiate with the team, but you are best to address the elephant in the room.

Take a moment to reflect on your promises or commitments, and address how much trust is in the bank with each of your team members.

LEADERS FORGIVE QUICKLY

Nothing is more unpleasant than a leader with a chip on their shoulder. Forgiveness is a subject personal to everyone. Some people do not forgive easily; others allow themselves to be trampled on unnecessarily. I have met many team members who will never forgive. If anyone crosses them, there is no way back. They are forever removed from the Christmas card list. In my view, life is too short for unforgiveness. I choose not to allow people to rent space in my mind where the walls are painted the colour of resentment. No one is that important.

You may say, "That's easy for you to say; you don't know what they did to me." I'm afraid I have to disagree. You don't know my story, and I don't know yours. Often, when I walk through security at an airport and the alarms go off, I quietly think that must be all the knives in my back from a life in leadership. I have been criticised, slandered, betrayed, and disliked personally and professionally. I have reached out to a father who disowned me, been called as a witness for the prosecution at his criminal court case, and was judged by his friends when I arranged his funeral and paid for his burial costs.

May I be honest with you? We will all suffer offence, heartbreak, and distress. No one is immune. If others haven't hurt you, be patient; your time will come. It is not what happens to you that matters. The important thing is how you respond. Here are some helpful points.

Forgiveness is not forgetfulness.

Just because you forgive doesn't mean you forget. If I lend money to a friend, and they don't repay, I may choose to forgive the debt. But do you think I will lend money again? Probably not. I'm not giving a bank robber keys to the safe.

Sometimes, it's okay to part company.

Some people think forgiveness means everything goes back to normal. Not necessarily so. If an employee steals from you or acts unprofessionally in the workplace, make sure you forgive them after firing them. I chose to set boundaries with my father and forgive him. But I knew giving him open access to my family would be harmful.

Forgiveness does not mean validating bad behaviour.

I forgave my father yet testified against him in his court case. His victims deserved justice. Don't feel the need to validate bad behaviour by offering forgiveness. Even the Scriptures tell us that justice belongs to God, and He will repay. Forgiving someone is simply saying I choose to let this offence go. You will stand before a higher power one day, but that's not me.

Forgiveness is best seen as the release of a debt.

The famous prayer Jesus taught his disciples includes, "Forgive us our debts as we forgive our debtors". I have chosen to forgive debts. I am not owed an apology. To be honest, I am not completely innocent either. I am acutely aware of my own failings. How can I expect forgiveness if I am unwilling to offer it to others?

Leaders forgive quickly.

FINAL WORDS

Thank you for taking the time to read my thoughts on leadership. My hope for you is that you will truly become a legacy leader and that you will be remembered positively by those you meet on this wonderful adventure called life.

I am convinced that you were born to make a positive difference in the lives of others, and regardless of age, it is not too soon or too late to begin living your legacy life.

I offer you my best wishes and thoughts for your future.

I always welcome communication if you would like to get in touch.

Graeme Lauridsen.

www.ingramcontent.com/pod-product-compliance
Lightning Source LLC
Chambersburg PA
CBHW020846210326
41597CB00041B/1011